Cavendish

The Laws of Piquet Adopted by the Portland and Turf Clubs

Ninth Edition

Cavendish

The Laws of Piquet Adopted by the Portland and Turf Clubs
Ninth Edition

ISBN/EAN: 9783744733915

Printed in Europe, USA, Canada, Australia, Japan

Cover: Foto ©ninafisch / pixelio.de

More available books at **www.hansebooks.com**

THE LAWS

OF

PIQUET

ADOPTED BY

THE PORTLAND AND TURF CLUBS

WITH

A TREATISE ON THE GAME

BY

"CAVENDISH"

AUTHOR OF
"THE LAWS AND PRINCIPLES OF WHIST"
ETC., ETC.

NINTH EDITION.

LONDON:
THOMAS DE LA RUE & CO.
1896.

The following Clubs have given their adhesion to the Piquet Laws adopted by the PORTLAND and TURF CLUBS, viz.:—

ARMY AND NAVY.

CONSERVATIVE.

GUARDS.

JUNIOR ATHENÆUM.

MARLBOROUGH.

NEW UNIVERSITY.

OXFORD AND CAMBRIDGE.

REFORM.

ST. JAMES'S WHIST.

UNION.

UNITED UNIVERSITY.

UNITED WHIST.

WINDHAM.

CONTENTS.

	PAGE
PREFACE	ix
THE LAWS OF PIQUET	1
LAWS OF PIQUET *AU CENT*	16
CASES AND DECISIONS	21

TREATISE ON PIQUET.

PREFACE	41
HISTORICAL	43

DESCRIPTION OF THE GAME.

INTRODUCTORY	83
DEALING	83
DISCARDING	83
CALLING AND SHOWING	86
PLAYING	93
CARTE BLANCHE, PIQUE AND REPIQUE	95
SCORING	97
EXAMPLE	103

CHOUETTE PIQUET 106

CONDUCT OF THE GAME.

SHUFFLING	107
DEALING	108
MANAGEMENT OF THE STOCK	108
TAKING UP THE HAND	108
TAKING IN	108
CALLING AND SHOWING	109
PLAYING THE CARDS	112
SCORING	115

DISCARDING.

	PAGE
INTRODUCTORY	116
GENERAL RULES	116
CALCULATIONS	121
EXAMPLES	125

CALLING.

INTRODUCTORY	152
CALLING THE POINT	152
REPLYING TO THE CALL OF POINT . . .	154
CALLING SEQUENCES	156
SINKING	156
EXAMPLES OF SINKING	158

PLAYING THE CARDS.

COUNTING THE HAND	166
HABIT OF ADVERSARY	167
PLAYING TO OBTAIN INFORMATION . . .	168
ESTABLISHING A SUIT	169
PRESERVING GUARDS AND TENACES . . .	169
PLAYING TO SAVE A CAPOT	170
PLAYING TO THE SCORE	171
EXAMPLES	174

ODDS AT PIQUET.

THE SHOW	203
ODDS AT VARIOUS SCORES	204
NEGLECTED VARIATIONS	207
ODDS IRRESPECTIVE OF THE TABLES . . .	208

PREFACE.

At the Annual General Meeting of the PORTLAND CLUB, held February 24th, 1881, it was unanimously resolved that a Committee be appointed to draw up Laws of Piquet. The following gentlemen were nominated, and kindly consented to serve:—

JOHN SAMUEL, Esq.
(Chairman).

HENRY JONES, Esq. | SAMUEL SMITH, Esq.
M. TREVELYAN MARTIN, Esq. | ROBERT WHEBLE, Esq.

The Committee having drawn up a Code, submitted it to the TURF CLUB. A Committee was appointed by the TURF CLUB, consisting of the following gentlemen, who agreed to serve:—

The Hon. HENRY LEESON.
Major The Hon. OLIVER G. P. MONTAGU.
FREDERIC NORRIS, Esq.

The TURF Committee proposed a few amendments; and, after further deliberation and discussion, the two Committees sanctioned the publication of the Laws that follow.

PORTLAND CLUB,
    January, 1882.

LAWS OF PIQUET.

THE LAWS OF PIQUET.

SHUFFLING.

1. Each player has a right to shuffle both his own and his adversary's pack. The dealer has the right of shuffling last.

2. The pack must not be shuffled below the table, nor in such manner as to expose the faces of any of the cards.

CUTTING.

3. A cut must consist of at least two cards, and at least two must be left in the lower packet.

4. In cutting, the ace is highest. The player who cuts the higher card has the choice of deal, and the dealer has the choice of cards at the commencement of each partie.

5. If, in cutting for deal, a player expose more than one card, he must cut again.

6. The cut for the deal holds good, even if the pack be incorrect.

7. If, in cutting to the dealer, or in reuniting the separated packets, a card be exposed, or if there be any confusion of the cards, there must be a fresh cut.

8. When a player in cutting has once separated the pack, he must abide by the cut.

DEALING.

9. The dealer must deal the cards by two at a time or by three at a time, giving the top cards to his adversary, the next to himself, and so on, until each player has twelve cards. The dealer having selected the mode in which he will distribute the cards, must not change it during the partie. The eight undealt cards (called the stock) are to be placed face downward, in one packet, on the table between the players.

10. If the dealer deal the cards wrongly, he may, with the permission of his adversary, rectify the error prior to either player having taken up his hand.

11. If the elder hand find that he has a card too many or a card too few, he has the option of a fresh deal after looking at his hand, but before taking up a card of the stock. If the elder hand, having twelve cards dealt him, find, in drawing the stock toward him after discarding, that it contains but seven cards, he has the option of a fresh deal, or of altering his discard.

12. If more than one card be dealt wrongly, or if there be nine cards in the stock, there must be a fresh deal (except as provided in Law 10).

13. If the dealer expose a card belonging to his adversary, or to the stock, the elder hand has the option of a fresh deal. If the dealer expose any of his own cards, the deal stands good.

14. If a faced card be found in the pack when dealing, or in the stock when taking in, there must be a fresh deal.

15. If the dealer deal with the wrong pack, and the error be discovered before either player has taken up any of his cards, there must be a fresh deal with the right pack. If the error be not discovered before either player has taken up any of his cards, the deal holds good, and the packs remain changed.

16. The players deal alternately. If a player deal out of his turn, and either player discover the error before taking up any of his cards, the deal in error is void, and the right dealer deals. But if the error be discovered too late to correct it, the elder hand in that deal must deal twice running with the same pack (except as provided in Law 76), unless that or the next deal be the last of the partie.

17. The non-dealer must collect the cards for the ensuing deal, and must place them, properly collected, face downward on the table.

CARTE BLANCHE.

18. Carte blanche (*i.e.*, a hand dealt, consisting of at least twelve cards, without king, queen, or knave) scores first, and consequently saves a pique or a repique. It also counts toward a pique or a repique.

19. Carte blanche must be shown by counting the cards, one by one, face upward on the table.

20. As soon as a player is aware that he has a carte blanche, he is bound to inform his adversary, but he need not show the carte blanche until his adversary has discarded.

DISCARDING AND TAKING IN.

21. The elder hand is entitled to discard five cards and to take in five. He is obliged to discard one card (except as provided in Law 42).

22. The younger hand is entitled to discard three cards, and to take in three (except as provided in Laws 41 and 43). He is obliged to discard one card (except as provided in Law 40).

23. In taking in, the cards must be taken in order from the top of the stock.

24. After a player has taken up a card of the stock he cannot alter his discard.

25. If a player, after having taken up a card of the stock, take back into his hand any of his discard, he must play with more than twelve cards, and can reckon nothing that deal.

26. If a player, after having taken up a card of the stock, mix any of his hand, or any card he is entitled to take in, with his discard, he must leave it with his discard. He must play with less than twelve cards, and his adversary counts as tricks all cards that cannot be played to.

27. If the elder hand, when taking in, or when looking at cards he has left, expose or take up any of the bottom three cards of the stock (except as provided in Laws 41 and 43), he can

reckon nothing that deal. And similarly, if the younger hand, when taking in, expose or take up any of the top five cards of the stock (not being cards declared to be left by the elder hand), he can reckon nothing that deal.

28. If the elder hand mix with his hand any of the bottom three cards of the stock (except as provided in Laws 41 and 43), or if, having left any cards, he mix with his hand any of the cards he ought to have left, he can reckon nothing that deal; or, the younger hand, after looking at his hand, may elect to have a fresh deal. If he elect to stand the deal, he can only take as many of his cards as have not been mixed.

29. If the younger hand mix with his hand any of the top five cards of the stock (not being cards declared to be left by the elder hand), he can reckon nothing that deal; or, the elder hand, after looking at his .hand, may elect to have a fresh deal. If he elect to stand the deal, he can only take as many of his cards as have not been mixed. If, however, the elder hand have taken in some of his cards, the others remaining on the stock, and the younger hand take up any of them, he incurs no penalty, unless he mix any of the cards taken up with his hand, when he can reckon nothing that deal.

30. If a player, having twelve cards dealt him, discard more cards than he takes in, he must play with less than twelve cards, and his adversary counts as tricks all cards that cannot be played to.

31. If a player, having twelve cards dealt him, take in more cards than he discards, but do not take from the stock one of his adversary's cards, he must play with more than twelve cards, and can reckon nothing that deal.

32. If the elder hand do not take all his cards, he must declare the number he takes or leaves before taking up a card of the stock. If he fail to do so, and the younger hand, on touching the stock (but before taking up a card of it), find that it contains more than three cards, he is entitled to alter his discard, and to take in the card or cards left.

33. If the elder hand leave any cards, he is entitled to look at them; but if he take them up, together with the cards he is about to take in, he can reckon nothing that deal.

34. The younger hand is entitled to take in all the cards that are left in the stock.

35. If the younger hand leave any cards, and take up, together with the cards he is about to take in, more cards than he has discarded, he can reckon nothing that deal.

36. If the younger hand leave any cards he is entitled to see them; but he must declare whether he will look at them or not, after the elder hand has named the suit he will first lead, or has led a card, and before playing a card himself. If the younger hand elect to look at them, the elder hand is also entitled to see them, after he has named the suit he will first lead, or has led a

THE LAWS OF PIQUET. 7

card. If the younger hand elect not to look at them, neither player has a right to see them.

37. If the younger hand leave any cards, and mix them with his discard without showing them to the elder hand, the elder hand, after leading a card, is entitled to see his adversary's discard, and the cards mixed with it.

38. If a player announce that he has eleven or thirteen cards dealt him, the stock may be counted to ascertain how many cards it contains.

39. If the elder hand, having eleven or thirteen cards dealt him, take up a card of the stock without announcing the error, he loses his option of a fresh deal. He cannot alter his discard, and he must leave at least three cards for the younger hand. But, if the stock contain seven cards, and the elder hand have eleven, there must be a fresh deal.

40. If the elder hand elect to stand the deal when he has thirteen cards, and there are eight in the stock, he must discard one card more than he takes in, and he must discard at least two cards. The younger hand must discard one less than he takes in; but, if he only take one card, he need not discard any.

41. If the elder hand elect to stand the deal when he has thirteen cards, and there are seven in the stock, he must discard one more card than he takes in. He must discard at least two cards; and, if he take all his cards, he discards six, and the younger hand can only take two cards.

42. If the elder hand elect to stand the deal when he has eleven cards, and there are eight in the stock, he must discard one less than he takes in; but, if he only take one card, he need not discard any. The younger hand must discard one more than he takes in, and he must discard at least two cards.

43. If the elder hand elect to stand the deal when he has twelve cards, and there are seven in the stock, he must discard the same number of cards as he takes in; and, if he take all his cards, the younger hand can only take two cards. The younger hand must discard one more than he takes in, and he must discard at least two cards.

44. When a player subjects himself to the penalty of reckoning nothing that deal, the adversary has the option of not enforcing the penalty.

45. A player may examine his own discard at any time.

CALLING AND SHOWING

46. The elder hand must call his point first, or he loses the right to call it. It is sufficient to call the number of cards of the point. The younger hand is not entitled to reply by inquiring what the elder hand's point makes, unless he hold at least an equal number of cards; and the inquiry bars him from counting a superior number of cards for point.

47. It is not compulsory on the younger hand to call his point first; nor is it compulsory on either player to call sequence next after point.

48. It is sufficient to call the number of cards of a sequence if the call be good against the cards. If not good against the cards, the elder hand is bound to state to what card his sequence is. And similarly, in calling a quatorze or trio, the elder hand is bound to state the value of the cards of which it consists, unless the call is good against the cards.

49. If the elder hand first call a sequence which is good against the cards, he can reckon any sequences he holds, whether of superior counting value to the one called or not. And similarly, if the elder hand first call a trio or a quatorze which is good against the cards, he can reckon any quatorzes or trios that he holds.

50. If the elder hand call a smaller point, sequence, quatorze, or trio than he holds, he may correct his miscall before it has been replied to by the younger hand.

51. If the younger hand allow a correct call to be good or equal, when he holds better in his hand, he may correct his reply before the elder hand has made another call; or, in case there is no further call, before the elder hand has led a card.

52. If either player call a larger point, sequence, quatorze, or trio than he holds, and it is allowed to be good, he may correct his miscall before the younger hand has played to the first trick. In case of a correction of such miscall by the younger hand, after the elder hand has led, the

elder hand is at liberty to retake the card he led, and to play differently.

53. There is no penalty for a misnomer. It is a misnomer, if a player call a point or sequence, when he holds one of that counting value, but names the suit wrongly; or a sequence, when he holds one of that counting value, but names its rank wrongly; or a trio or quatorze, when he holds one, but names its rank wrongly; provided, however, that he could not possibly have held what he claims, in his hand and discard taken together.

54. If a player who calls a point, sequence, quatorze, or trio that he does not hold, and such call is allowed to be good, do not correct his miscall before the younger hand has played to the first trick, he can reckon nothing that deal, except in the case of a misnomer, or of his having called anything which he could not possibly have held in his hand and discard taken together, when he is liable to no penalty. On discovery of the error, the adversary may reckon anything he has good, which is not barred by a correct call of the player in error, made in addition to his miscall.

55. A player who calls anything which is allowed to be good or equal, must show the cards called at any time they are asked for, or in the case of the younger hand, at any time after the elder hand has led a card. If a player, before he plays a card, voluntarily show anything which he claims to be good or equal, he is liable to no penalty for miscalling what he has shown.

56. When the younger hand has played to the first trick, neither player can reckon anything omitted (except as provided in Law 54).

PLAYING.

57. If a player play with less than twelve cards in hand, he is liable to no penalty. His adversary counts as tricks all cards that cannot be played to.

58. If a player play with more than twelve cards in hand, he can reckon nothing that deal; but his cards, though not good to score, are good to bar his adversary.

59. A card once led or played cannot be taken up, except as provided in Law 52, and as follows:—

I. If a player accidentally drop a card or cards, he may retake them.

II. If the leader lead two or more cards consecutively without waiting for his adversary to play, and the adversary play too many cards, he may, on discovery of the error, retake the extra card or cards. All cards subsequently played in error must be taken up and played over again.

III. If a player lead out of turn, the card led may be taken up, unless the adversary have played to the trick, when the error cannot be rectified.

IV. If a player do not follow suit when able, he must, when the error is detected, retake any cards played in error, and substitute the suit led. The players also retake all cards played after the mistake, and the play of the remainder of the cards then proceeds as though no error had been committed.

V. If a player, when asked what cards he has in hand which have been allowed to be good or equal, misinform his adversary, the adversary may retake all cards played subsequently to the misinformation, and play differently.

60. A player is entitled to examine both his own and his adversary's tricks at any time.

SCORING.

61. Carte blanche scores ten.

62. The largest point is good. The point, when good, scores one for each card.

63. The longest sequence is good; as between sequences of equal length the highest is good. Sequences, when good, score as follows: a huitième scores eighteen; a septième, seventeen; a sixième, sixteen; a quint, fifteen; a quart, four; a tierce, three.

64. The highest quatorze is good. Any quatorze is good against a trio. As between trios, the highest trio is good. A quatorze, when good, scores fourteen. A trio, when good, scores three.

65. In playing the cards, each player scores one for every card he leads, or with which he wins a trick. The winner of the last trick scores two instead of one.

66. A player who wins more than six tricks scores ten for the cards. If each player win six tricks the cards are divided, and there is no score for them. A player who wins twelve tricks wins a capot, and scores forty for the cards instead of ten.

67. The scores, whether obtained by the elder or younger hand, reckon in the following order:—

   I. Carte blanche.
   II. Point.
   III. Sequences.
   IV. Quatorzes and trios.
   V. Points made in play.
   VI. The cards.

68. A repique is obtained on the score of thirty being made by a player, in his hand alone, by scores that reckon in order before anything that his adversary can count. A player obtaining a repique adds sixty to his score.

69. A pique is obtained on the score of thirty being made by the elder hand, in hand and play, before his adversary has reckoned anything that deal. A player obtaining a pique adds thirty to his score. A capot reckons after points made in play; and, therefore, does not count toward a pique.

70. Errors in counting the hand, if proved, may be rectified at any time before the player in error has seen his next hand.

71. A partie consists of six deals. The partie is won by the player who makes the higher score in six deals. If both players score the same number in six deals, each deals once more, when the partie is concluded, even if there should be a second tie.

NOTE.—By agreement, a partie may consist of four deals, the score in the first and last deals counting double. In case of a tie, each deals once more, the scores in the extra deals counting single.

72. The winner of the partie deducts the score of the loser from his own; and the difference, with a hundred added, is the number of points won.

73. If the loser fail to score a hundred, the winner, whether his score reach a hundred or not, adds the score of the loser to his own; and the sum, with a hundred added, is the number of points won.

74. In case of a difference in the written scores, a player's score of his own hand shall be taken as correct.

INCORRECT PACKS.

75. If a pack be discovered to be incorrect, redundant, or imperfect, the deal in which the discovery is made is void. All preceding deals stand good.

CHANGING CARDS.

76. Before the pack is cut to the dealer a player may call for fresh cards at his own expense. He must call for two new packs, of which the dealer has the choice.

77. Torn or marked cards must be replaced, or new packs called for at the expense of the two players.

BYSTANDERS.

78. If a bystander call attention to any error or oversight, and thereby affect the score, he may be called on to pay all stakes and bets of the player whose interest he has prejudicially affected.

LAWS OF PIQUET AU CENT.

The Laws of Piquet *au cent*, differ from those of Piquet in the following particulars:—The player who cuts the lower card has to deal. If he expose more than one card in cutting, his adversary may treat the lowest of the exposed cards as the one cut.

The deal is by two cards at a time.

If the elder hand find that he has a card too many or too few, he has the option of a fresh deal before touching the stock.

If the dealer deal with the wrong pack, and the error be discovered before the deal is completed, there must be a fresh deal with the right pack. If not discovered before the deal is completed, the deal holds good.

If a player deal out of his turn, and discover his error before taking up his hand, the deal in error is void, and the right dealer deals. If not discovered before taking up the hand, there is no remedy.

If the younger hand have a carte blanche, he need not declare it until his adversary has discarded and touched the stock.

The younger hand is not obliged to discard any card.

After a player has touched the stock he cannot alter his discard (except as provided in Laws of Piquet 11, 32, and 38).

If the elder hand mix with his hand one of the three bottom cards of the stock, he loses the game; and, similarly, if the elder hand, having left a card or cards, mix with his hand any of the cards he ought to have left, he loses the game.

If the younger hand take up any of the top five cards of the stock (not being cards declared to be left by the elder hand), he loses the game.

If the elder hand do not take all his cards, he must declare the number he takes or leaves before touching the stock.

If the younger hand leave any cards and elect not to look at them, and either player should then look at them, they must be exposed, and a suit may be called from the offender when next he has to lead.

If the elder hand elect to stand the deal when he has thirteen cards, he must discard one more card than he takes in, but he is not obliged to take in any. He must leave at least three cards for the younger hand.

If the elder hand elect to stand the deal when he has eleven cards and there are eight in the stock, he must discard one less than he takes in, and he must discard one card. The younger hand must discard one more than he takes in, but he is not obliged to take in any. If the elder hand elect to stand the deal when he has twelve cards and there are seven in the stock, he must leave at least three cards for the younger hand. The younger hand must discard one more than he takes in, but he is not obliged to take in any.

The elder hand must call the number his point makes. It is not sufficient to call the number of cards of the point.

It is not sufficient to call the number of cards of a sequence. The elder hand must state to what card his sequence is. And, similarly, if he call a quatorze or trio, he is bound to state the value of the cards of which it consists.

If the elder hand call a smaller point, sequence, quatorze or trio than he holds, or a trio when he holds a quatorze, he must abide by his call, and he cannot reckon anything superior, even though his call is good against the cards. He may, however, correct a misnomer of sequence, trio, or quatorze, before he leads a card, and may reckon anything of equal or inferior counting value, provided his call in error was good against the cards.

The elder hand having called anything which is good or equal must show the cards called, except in the case of quatorzes and trios. If he lead a card without showing his call, he cannot reckon it, and the adversary may show and reckon his point or sequence, even though it be equal or inferior to the one called.

If the elder hand show a sequence and call an inferior one, he cannot reckon the superior one; but the show bars the younger hand from reckoning his sequences, if only equal or inferior to the one shown.

The younger hand having allowed a correct call to be good or equal, must abide by his answer.

If the younger hand disallow a call, and it be discovered that the call of the elder hand is good or equal, the elder hand can show and reckon his superiority, or show his equality, notwithstanding that he has led a card.

If the younger hand say equal or not good to a call, and play to the first trick without showing his superiority or equality, the elder may show and reckon what he has called, notwithstanding that he has led a card.

If a player call a quatorze or trio which he does not hold, and it is allowed to be good, and he play a card without correcting the miscall, he can reckon nothing that deal.

When the elder hand has led a card, or the younger hand played to a trick, they cannot reckon anything omitted.

By agreement, points ending in four count one less than the number of cards.

By agreement, in playing the cards, nines, eights, and sevens are not counting cards.

Errors in adding up, or in marking the score, if proved, may be rectified at any time during the game.

A game is one hundred up. A player scoring a hundred before his adversary has scored fifty wins a double game.

A partie is won by a player who wins three games out of five, a double counting as two games.

A player has no choice of cards on commencing a fresh partie.

CASES AND DECISIONS.

Case I.

A calls four cards for point. B replies, "Equal." A says, "Forty-one." B then finds he cannot have a point of forty-one, but that he has a point of five cards. A claims to score the point.

Decision.—A cannot score the point. He has not made another call or a further call (Law 51); he has only completed an imperfect call.

B's reply bars him from counting a superior number of cards for point (Law 46). His point, though not good to score, is good to save a pique or a repique.

Case II.

A calls three kings, which B allows to be good. It is presently discovered that A has not three kings. B then claims to reckon four tens. Is he entitled to do so?

Decision.—Yes. B's admission of three kings being good is subject to A's holding them. B, it is true, might at once have disallowed the call; but, when he supposes A to have three kings, he may desire to sink his tens, and this he may no longer wish to do if he knows A to have a king out.

Case III.

A proposes a fresh deal.

B makes no reply until after A has discarded, when he says he will give a fresh deal.

A, judging from B's hesitation that there is not a powerful hand against him, states that he does not now wish for a fresh deal. B insists that as he has never refused the offer, it is still open.

Decision.—The law does not contemplate the offer of a fresh deal. A fresh deal is a matter of agreement between the players. In this case, though B has not, in words, refused a fresh deal, he has allowed A to carry the game a step further by discarding. This is tantamount to a refusal.

Case IV.

A calls a point headed by ace, and two tierce majors in other suits, and leads a card, but says nothing about aces. Can B reckon three knaves?

Decision.—B cannot reckon three knaves. A has declared three aces by implication, and can reckon anything he has omitted before B plays to the first trick (Law 56). B's course is to play a card, saying nothing about knaves, when A loses the score for the aces.

If, however, A is under a rubicon, and B calls knaves, if A objects he must reckon his aces.

Case V.

Elder hand directs the younger to discard for carte blanche. The younger having discarded three cards, the elder then shows his hand, and says, "I leave a card." Can the younger hand alter his discard after having seen his adversary's cards?

Decision.—Yes. The elder hand should state that he leaves a card before showing his carte blanche.

Case VI.

Elder hand discards, and takes up a card of the stock (Law 24).

Younger hand then finds he has a carte blanche, and proposes to show it (Law 19).

Can the elder hand alter his discard, as he has not been informed of the carte blanche? (Law 20.)

If not, can the younger hand reckon the carte blanche, as he has not informed the elder hand in time for him to discard for a carte blanche?

Decision.—The elder hand cannot alter his discard. The younger hand can reckon the carte blanche.

Note.—This is a matter of etiquette rather than of law. The younger hand is bound to inform the elder as soon as he is aware he has a carte blanche (Law 20). If he is not aware that he has a carte blanche before the elder has taken up a card of the stock, there is no help for it.

The younger hand cannot be required to do an impossibility. Of course, *bona fides* is assumed on the part of the younger hand, *i.e.*, that he has not unnecessarily delayed his declaration.

The old law was that the younger hand need not inform the elder of a carte blanche. The distinction between the duties of the elder and younger hands in this respect, was no doubt drawn in order to preclude the occurrence of such a case as the present.

Case VII.

A calls three queens. B says, "Which queen do you not reckon?" A replies, "Queen of diamonds," and then reckons queens. B says, "Three queens are not good; I have three kings." Is B entitled to score his kings?

Decision.—No. Asking which queen is out is equivalent to admitting three queens to be good. B, by ascertaining which queen is out, obtains information to which he is only entitled in the case of A's scoring the queens.

Case VIII.

A calls three kings. B says, "Good. Which king do you not reckon?" A replies, "King of diamonds." On playing the cards it is discovered that A has the king of diamonds in hand, and that he has put out the king of hearts.

B claims that A can score nothing that hand. A contends that it is only a misnomer, for which he cannot be punished.

Decision.—B's claim is correct. It is true that A actually held three kings; but, as the reply of the elder hand is only a substitute for showing the kings, he has defined his claim to be for three kings, including one which he has not got. He is therefore liable to the penalty for scoring what he does not hold.

Case IX.

A calls four knaves (holding only three). B replies, "Good." A then says, "I beg your pardon, I have only three knaves." B replies, "Not good." B might have held four aces, but, having discarded an ace, has only three.

A thus discovers before he leads a card that B has an ace out, and so obtains information to which he is not entitled. Has B any remedy?

Decision.—B has no remedy. It is one of those accidents that will occasionally happen which card laws cannot reach.

Case X.

A (elder hand) has a quint major, and such other cards that he will probably put B to a card. A places the quint major on the table and says, "Play five cards."

B accidentally plays six cards.

At the end of the hand, when A plays his last card, it is found that B has no card to play to it.

B claims to play the hand over again (Law 59, par. II.)

A urges that B was distinctly informed how many cards he had to play; that he cannot benefit by his own mistake; and that, now he has seen all the cards, he knows which card to keep in order to save the capot.

Decision.—The hand must be played over again, B retaking one of the cards he played to the quint major.

A might have protected himself by counting the cards originally played by B. If he is too careless to do so, he must take the consequences.

Case XI.

A (elder hand), having a quint major in clubs and the seven, places the quint major on the table together with the seven of spades, and says, "Play six cards."

B plays five cards, and then takes the seven of spades with the eight. A then says, "I made a mistake; I intended to have played the seven of clubs." Can A rectify his error?

Decision.—A is too late after B has played his sixth card. But prior to that A can rectify his error.

Case XII.

A (elder hand), has a tierce to a knave in clubs, good against the cards. He might also have had a tierce to a queen in hearts, but he has discarded from that suit. He calls a point in diamonds, and a tierce, but does not declare in what suit it is, nor to what card it is (Law 48). B (younger hand), plays on the supposition that the tierce is in hearts, and in consequence loses the cards. B then claims to play the cards again, on the ground that he has been misinformed (Law 59, par. V.), or, at least, that he has not been sufficiently informed.

Decision.—B has not been misinformed, and has no right to have the cards played again. He might have protected himself by asking A to show the tierce (Law 55), or, what amounts to the same thing, by asking to what card the tierce is.

Note.—As a matter of etiquette, it is usual among piquet players to volunteer information when there may be a doubt as to the nature of the claim. Thus the younger hand might have the point, good or equal, in more than one suit. After the elder hand has led a card, it would be in accordance with custom for him to say " In hearts," or whatever the suit may be; or, if he has a high card of his point out that might influence the play (his point nevertheless being good or equal), to show the cards.

In case no mention is made of the suit, the claim is generally understood, among players, to refer to the highest or best combination that can be held, in the case of the tierces, first given, to the tierce to a queen. If A and B are in the habit of playing on that tacit understanding, B has just cause of complaint, and A should endeavour to repair the injury inflicted on B, the simplest course probably being not to demur to B's request to play the cards again.

Similar observations apply to quatorzes and trios. Thus the elder hand has point and quart, both good, and might also have three kings and three tens, both good against the cards, but has put out a king. He should not call his hand thus:—"Five and four are nine, and three are twelve." He should say, "and three tens are twelve."

Case XIII.

B (younger hand) accidentally takes up a card less than he discards. The mistake is discovered when the hand has been partly played out. B claims to take in the card he left on the table, the card in question not having been mixed with his discard.

Decision.—B can take up the card he left on the table, unless he has announced that he will leave a card, when he must play with eleven cards. If B has not renounced in the suit to which the card belongs, the hand proceeds in the usual way. If he has renounced, Law 59, par. IV., comes into operation.

Case XIV.

The younger hand (B) discards and takes up the bottom three cards of the stock before the elder hand (A) has taken in. A then says, "I leave a card." What is the consequence?

Decision.—B having taken up a card of the stock cannot alter his discard; and, as in taking in he is obliged to take the cards in order from the top of the stock, including cards left by the elder hand, he must take the card left by A, must play with thirteen cards, and can reckon nothing that deal.

Case XV.

The elder hand holds king, knave, ten, nine, eight, seven of diamonds. He calls six cards which are not good, and a quint minor which is good.

During the play of the cards, the elder throws ten, nine, eight, seven of diamonds. The younger hand then says, "How many diamonds?" The elder replies, "Two." The younger, supposing that the reply is only as regards the quint, plays accordingly and loses the cards thereby. He then claims to play the end of the hand again under Law 59, par. V.

Decision.—The question can only be asked with regard to cards reckoned for or called as equal. The reply, therefore, can only be with regard to those cards. The younger hand has been misinformed, and can claim to play the end of the hand again.

Note.—This decision has been much disputed. Compare Case XVI.

Case XVI.

In the contrary case, of a player's replying "One" (or whatever the number may be), when he has more which he has not declared, the adversary must take the reply to be in respect of cards reckoned as good or declared as equal.

For example :—B (younger hand), who has discarded at least one spade, remains with three cards in hand, viz., ace, queen of hearts, and king of spades. He has not declared any point, aces, or queens, but has reckoned a quart minor in hearts. A (elder hand) has ace, queen of spades, and king of hearts. Before leading, he says, "How many hearts?" B replies, "None." No one disputes that B is justified in this, and that his reply is understood, by all piquet players, to mean, "None that I have declared."

Note.—In both this and the previous case the question put is irregular. It should strictly take this form, "How many of your quint?" or, "How many of your quart?" as the case may be. Or, the request may be, "Show me anything you have declared" (Law 55). But as the irregularity is permitted by custom, it is assumed that the player who has to answer will frame his reply with reference only to cards called as good or declared as equal. This consideration guides the decision in Case XV.

Case XVII.

A has thirteen cards in his hand. He does not notice it, but discards five cards and takes in five. After he has taken in it is discovered that he has in his discard a card belonging to the undealt pack. A claims a fresh deal under Law 75.

Decision.—There is no proof that when the pack was dealt it was redundant. The surplus card may have got into A's hand or discard after the deal was completed. A is liable to the penalty for playing with thirteen cards, and can reckon nothing that deal.

Case XVIII.

The facts are as in the previous case; but A keeps in his hand the card belonging to the undealt pack instead of discarding it.

Decision.—In this case, if A has not played the surplus card he may return it to the undealt pack, and there is no penalty, unless A has used this card in scoring anything that is allowed to be good, or in showing anything that is allowed to be equal, and has afterwards led a card. He is then liable to the penalty for an unfounded claim, and can reckon nothing that deal) subject however to the possibility of his having held what he claims, in his hand and discard taken together, as provided in Law 54).

If the surplus card has been played prior to the discovery of the error, the hands must be taken up and played over again, the surplus card being first removed.

Case XIX.

A plays with thirteen cards; B with twelve.

B wins the twelfth trick, and scores two for it.

A objects that the twelfth trick is not the last trick (Law 65), and that his thirteenth card, though not good to score, is good to bar the adversary (Law 58).

Decision.—The word "last," in Law 65, presupposes that each player has twelve cards. B is entitled to score two for the twelfth trick.

Case XX.

A says, "Discard for carte blanche." While B is considering what he will put out, A places his discard face downwards on the table, and takes up some cards of the stock. Can A then show his carte blanche?

Decision.—Yes, provided he has not mixed any of the stock with his hand. He must show his hand and his discard separately, as, having taken up a card of the stock, he must not retake any card of his discard.

Case XXI.

In continuation of the former case, B, on seeing A take up a card of the stock, says, "You have not shown your carte blanche." A replies, "No more I have," relinquishes the stock, mixes his discard with his hand, and is about to show the carte blanche, when B objects, that A having taken up a card of the stock, and then retaken his discard, must play with seventeen cards, and can reckon nothing that deal.

Decision.—B's contention is so far correct that A can reckon nothing after the carte blanche, which (so long as he has not mixed any of the stock with his hand) he is still at liberty to show and reckon. This score accrues before the play of the hand commences, and before any cards are taken in. Consequently, the law which bars a player from reckoning anything if he plays with too many cards does not apply to a carte blanche.

Case XXII.

It is the last hand of a partie. A (elder hand) is sixty-two. B (younger hand) is ninety-two.

A holds ace, king, queen, knave, nine of spades; king, knave of hearts; knave of clubs; and ace, queen, knave, ten of diamonds.

He has discarded eight, seven of hearts; eight, seven of clubs; and seven of diamonds.

B holds ten of spades; ace, queen, ten, nine of hearts; ace, king, queen, ten, nine of clubs; and king, nine, eight of diamonds (thirteen cards).

By mistake, he has only discarded two cards, viz., eight, seven of spades; and he has taken up together the three cards left in the stock. As he cannot alter his discard (Law 24), he is obliged to play with thirteen cards, and can reckon nothing that deal (Law 35).

The elder hand calls five cards, making fifty. The point is equal. The elder then calls a quart major, a tierce to a queen, and four knaves, good for twenty-one, and leads five spades. To these the younger hand plays ten of spades; nine, ten, queen of hearts, and eight of diamonds.

It matters not now what the elder hand leads. As the cards happen to lie, he scores most by leading king of hearts. B wins with the ace, and plays five clubs and divides the cards.

The scores are, A, 91; B (who reckons nothing), 92. B wins a rubicon (Law 73) of 283 points.

Now if B had played with twelve cards, he would have lost a rubicon. This is easily proved by taking from B's hand the card of least importance to him, say the eight of diamonds. A leads five spades, as before. It is immaterial what B plays. A must win at least the last two tricks, and the cards, and scores forty.

The scores are, A, 102; B, 98 (at most); but as probably B has seen he cannot save the rubicon, it may be taken that he has let A count thirteen in play, when the score will be, A, 106; B, 92. A wins a rubicon of 298 points.

Hence B profits, by his own blunder, to the amount of 581 points. The example is taken from actual play.

Similar examples could be furnished as to the call of a player, with thirteen cards, barring a pique or a repique, and as to the extra card saving a capot.

The penalty of scoring nothing that hand, when a player has too many cards, may not only be no penalty at all, but may give the player in fault an overwhelming advantage. That this should be possible is a serious blemish in the game; and it is suggested that it should be provided against by future legislators.

It is the fashion to say that, in the long run, the habitually careless player will lose more than he will gain, by playing with the wrong number of cards. This appears to the Author to amount merely to a lame excuse for an inadequate law.

A TREATISE ON PIQUET

BY

"CAVENDISH."

TO

THE MEMBERS

OF

THE PORTLAND CLUB

THIS

𝔗reatise on 𝔓iquet

IS

CORDIALLY DEDICATED.

PREFACE TO THE FIRST EDITION.

Since Hoyle's Treatise on Piquet was published in 1744, no original work on Piquet has appeared in the English language (so far as the author has been able to discover), though Hoyle has several times been edited with more or less success.

The issue of an authorized code of Laws* affords a good occasion for the publication of a fresh treatise on the game. Although the plan of it is original, the author has made free use of the examples contained in Hoyle's valuable work. The author has also (through the great kindness of Mr. Clay,) been able to avail himself of that accomplished player's judgment and experience. For the assistance rendered to him by Mr. Clay, the author takes this opportunity of expressing his warmest thanks.

PORTLAND CLUB,
May, 1873.

* Of Piquet *au cent*, by the Portland Club, in 1873 (and, *see* p. 81).

PIQUET.

HISTORICAL.

Numerous theories have been broached respecting the origin and etymology of Piquet; but no positive conclusions have been arrived at.

First as to the origin of the game. By some writers, of indifferent weight, it is referred to the period of the reign of Charles VI. (1380–1422).

Haydn ("Dictionary of Dates"), giving Mézéray as his authority, states that Piquet was the first known game on the cards and that it was invented by Joquemin for the amusement of Charles VI. of France. There is no such name as Joquemin to be found in any of the biographies. The person referred to is no doubt Jacquemin Gringonneur, to whom is erroneously ascribed the invention of playing cards in the reign of Charles VI. Some authorities are of opinion that Jacquemin was the name of a cardmaker, or *gringonneur* of that period, *gringonneur* signifying a maker of *grangons* (*certus tesserarum ludus*. Du Cange,

Glossary, Supplement, Vol. 11., col. 651). Persius ("*Rouge et Noir.* The Academicians of 1823." London. 1823.), says, "Of all the games at cards *Piquet* is the most ancient. * * * Its origin is somewhat singular; a great *Ballet* executed at the Court of Charles VI. suggested the idea of it."

He then describes the ballet. His description is identical with that of the interlude in *Le Triomphe des Dames*, printed in the *Théâtre François*, and danced some three hundred years later. He probably confuses one with the other.

It is now well ascertained that Piquet is by no means the most ancient of card games. Paul Boiteau d'Ambly ("*Les Cartes à jouer et la Cartomancie.*" Paris. 1854.), rebuts the idea that Piquet could have been played in the time of Charles VI. He writes, "*C'est au jeu de tarots que jouait Charles VI.* * * * *Ni le piquet ni, à plus forte raison le whist n'existaient.* * * * *Il n'y a de connu que le tarot.*"

The latest authorities are of opinion that tarot cards (*i.e.*, emblematic cards combined with numerals), were first used in Italy towards the end of the fourteenth century, and that soon afterwards the tarot game was subjected to the elimination of the emblematic series, leaving the numeral series to work by itself. It is, therefore, most unlikely that cards, with which Piquet could be played, were known in France as early as the time of Charles VI.

It is next attempted to fix the invention of Piquet on the period of Charles VII. (1422-1461); and, as this date is commonly upheld, especially by French writers, it is advisable to give a detailed account of their views.

In the "*Mémoire sur l'Origine du Jeu de Piquet trouvé dans l'Histoire de France, sous le Règne de Charles VII*", by Le Père Daniel (*Journal de Trévoux.* May, 1720.), Piquet is credited with being a symbolic, allegorical, military, political, and historical game. From the names of the personages on the court cards of early French packs, and from the marks of the suits, the Père believed he had made out the origin of Piquet, which he supposed to have been devised about 1430.

Chatto, a careful and sound critic ("Facts and Speculations on the Origin and History of Playing Cards." London. 1848.), speaks of Daniel's theories as "mere gratuitous conceits," and as the seethings of the father's imagination.

Saint-Foix ("*Essais Historiques sur Paris.*" Maestricht. 1778.), patronises the ballet theory. Referring to the interlude in *Le Triomphe des Dames*, he adds, "*Je crois que cet Intermede n'étoit pas nouveau, & qu'il n'étoit que l'esquisse d'un grand Ballet exécuté à la Cour de Charles VII, & sur lequel on eut idée du jeu du Piquet, qui certainement ne fut imaginé que vers la fin du règne de ce Prince.*"

Singer ("Researches into the History of Playing Cards." London. 1816.), follows Saint-Foix, but with great caution. He observes, "The game of Piquet appears to have been invented in the reign of Charles VII. It has been said that its invention took rise from a Ballet danced at the court of that Monarch; but it seems quite as probable, that this game furnished the device for the Ballet, as it has done at a later period."

Leber ("*Études historiques sur les Cartes à jouer.*" Paris. 1842.), agrees with Daniel in assigning a French origin to Piquet, in the time of Charles VII.

In Boiteau's "*Cartes à jouer*" there is a good deal of speculation as to the origin of Piquet. "*Rien de certain ne peut être avancé au sujet de ces commencements des cartes aux couleurs françaises et du jeu de piquet qui semble être né en même temps qu'elles. Le nom même du jeu ne s'explique pas facilement. Quoi qu'il en soit, les cartes aux couleurs cœur, carreau, pique et trèfle existent sous Charles VII et ne paraissent pas avoir été connues sous Charles VI. De plus, la création du jeu de piquet semble se rattacher par plus d'un lien au règne de Charles VII. Maintenant, Est-il possible d'admettre que tout à coup aient inventés ce jeu et ces cartes?* * * * *Dans les cent années qui vont de 1350 à 1450 il a dû s'introduire au milieu des cartes antiques plus d'une modification qui nous échappe.* * * * *C'est l'opinion de quelques personnes, qu'il a existé un jeu intermédiaire entre le tarot méridional ou allemand et le piquet français. De ce jeu intermédiaire il n'y a pas de traces, comme il n'y en a pas du travail qui a fait naitre le piquet. Il ne faut pas donc dire, comme M. Paul Lacroix, que le jeu de piquet est dû à la Hire* [the famous Stephen de Vignoles, a devoted adherent of Charles VII.] *ou à* *un servant d'armes de ce capitaine.* * * * *Il ne faut pas non plus accepter les prétendues explications des érudits du siècle dernier, qui ne sont, en général, que d'assez mauvaises conjectures. Ce sera dans les fêtes de Chinon, là où Charles VII perdait si gaiement son royaume, ce sera encore à Paris, après la victoire [1436] et dans la joie du triomphe, que la cour galante et militaire du roi sauvé par Jeanne d'Arc aura imaginé et oféré la réforme des cartes.* * * * *La France connaisait le tarot dans la seconde moitié du XIVe siècle.* * * * *La connaissance du jeu s'étant répandue, elle s'appliqua à approprier les cartes à son génie. La combinaison dite du jeu de piquet est née alors. C'est une simplification des élémens anciens. Les couleurs et le nombre des cartes, aussi bien que la création des règles fondamentales du jeu de piquet, datent de Charles VII et probablement du milieu de son règne, qui est aussi le milieu du XVe siècle. Jusqu'à ce moment, jusqu'au milieu du XVe siècle, l'histoire des cartes est enveloppée d'obscurités. La création du jeu français est la chose importante dans cette histoire.*"

Boiteau admits that nothing certain can be advanced on the subject of the origin of Piquet, and that just at the period of which he treats, the history of cards is wrapped in obscurity. After these admissions one may safely consign his theory to the region of guesses.

Dr. Willshire ("A descriptive Catalogue of Playing and other Cards in the British Museum."

London. 1876.), the most recent, and probably the best, authority, remarks that, "There is not satisfactory evidence * to show the date at which *piquet* was first played. * * * Endeavours have been made to associate the origin of this game with the epoch of Charles VII, but a decisive solution of the question cannot be obtained."

The supposition of Grosley ("*Mémoires historiques et critiques pour l'Histoire de Troyes.*" 1774.), that Piquet was invented by a mathematician of Troyes, named Picquet, who lived in the reign of Louis XIII. (1610–1643), and the statement of Strutt ("Sports and Pastimes." London. 1801.), that Piquet was introduced into France in the middle of the seventeenth century, may be met by reciting the fact that, about a century earlier, Rabelais (1535) includes Piquet in the list of games played by Gargantua. Boiteau believes that the Piquet mentioned by Rabelais was a different game; but this original notion requires confirmation.

Complex card games, like Piquet, are not invented by, nor for, individuals. They grow out of earlier and simpler games, until at last, through the survival of the fittest modifications, a highly developed game is evolved. As Boiteau well observes, "*Il est impossible de dire, prenant un jeu quelconque, qu'il a été inventé en telle année par un tel. C'est tantôt l'un et tantôt l'autre qui s'avise d'ajouter quelques règles à un vieux jeu, d'en changer le nom; des amis adoptent; quelques sociétés à la suite, et voilà une invention.*" It is therefore to the older card games that one should look for the origin of Piquet. The opinion of the latest writers on the history of playing cards is that France received her cards, and the games played with them, from Spain and Germany, and that these countries obtained them from Italy. If so, an examination of the early games and cards of Italy, Spain and Germany may throw some light on the question.

The ancient name of the point at Piquet was *ronfle*, and *la Ronfle* is one of the Gargantuan games mentioned by Rabelais (1535). There was also an Italian game called *Ronfa*, but it is not known how it was played. *Ronfa*, by some, is said to mean "ruff"; very likely this may be so, and the word ruffing may also mean discarding and taking in, as it did at the game of Ruff and Honours, an ancestor of whist. Berni ("*Capitolo del Gioco della Primiera col Commento di Messer Pietropaulo da San Chirico. Stampata in Roma nel Anno* M.D.XXVI."), includes *Ronfa* in a list of eleven card games, played at that time (1526).

In one place, the facetious commentator, who styles himself as above, thus refers to the invention of *Ronfa*. (The quotation is taken from Singer's translation.) "'We have but little certainty who was the inventor, or who, in the first instance developed the game, nor is that little confirmed by authority to be relied on. Some say it was Lorenzo de Medici the Magnificent, and relate I know not what tale of an Abbot. * * * Others will have it that Ferdinand of Naples, who so distinguished himself, was the inventor   Others Matthias, King of Hungary ; many Queen Isabella ; some the Grand Seneschal. * * * We shall leave the research to those who are desirous of knowing how many barrels of wine Acestes gave to Æneas ; or what was the name of Anchises' nurse ; and the like curiosities, worse than the Egg and Chicken.'"

Since *ronfle* was the point, and *ronfa* meant "ruff", and ruffing meant discarding and taking in from a stock, it is hardly too much to assume that *Ronfa* was a game in which discarding, taking in, and calling a point, were prominent features. *Ronfa* or *la Ronfle* may have been a simple form of Piquet ; or, the similarity of the words *ronfa, ronfle* and *ruff* may be mere coincidences.

When Italian cards, and the games played with them, travelled to Spain, a game called *Cientos* was played in that country. Singer says, "As this game was of Spanish original, and has some appearance of having resembled Piquet * * * may not the French have adopted it, with some alterations, merely changing its name?" Boiteau confirms the idea of the adoption thus :—" Le cent (*piquet*). *Le piquet s'appelle encore aujourd'hui le cent ou la grande brisque dans la Charente.*"

Singer assumes that the game originated in Spain. It is more probable that *Cientos* was a modified Italian game, possibly *Ronfa*, with a change of name.

From Spain or France the game came to England, where it was called Cent.

There is no similar record of a game like *Ronfa* or *Cientos* having reached Germany, when Italian cards journeyed to that part of Europe. The material leading to the supposition that such a game was played in Germany, whence it is geographically and historically probable it travelled to France, is very slender. What little there is depends on the amount of reliance to be placed on Merlin ("*Origine des Cartes à jouer.*" Paris. 1869.). The following quotation is taken from Willshire :—

"'We desired,'" "writes M. Merlin," "'to be able to point out in a satisfactory manner what were the names and structure of the [early] German games, but have not met with information precise enough on the subject. We must be contented with communicating a few remarks with which the examination of the cards has furnished us.

"'For figures we meet with kings, superior and inferior valets [the superior knave, *obermann*, is the equivalent of the queen in French and English packs]. * * *

"'The point cards are the ten, nine, eight, seven, six and two, a composition resembling our own *Piquet* [packs], in which the ace has been displaced by the two. This structure is * * *

that of the Saxon game *Schwerter Karte—cartes à l'épée*.

"'What appears to confirm our conjecture as to the analogy of *piquet* with this *jeu à l'épée*, is the fact that in the modern cards manufactured at Vienna for playing the German game, * * * the six is suppressed, as it is in the French *piquet* [pack] since the end of the seventeenth century.'"

It seems not improbable that an Italian game, bearing a likeness to Piquet, grew into *Cientos* in Spain and into *le Cent* in France; and, that a game played with sword packs, in which the number and value of the cards was the same as in piquet packs, was known in Germany; and that a modification of this Sword Game (to coin a name for it), afterwards found a home in France under the title of *Picquet* (the old spelling). But how, or when, the most advanced form of the older games finally established its supremacy as PIQUET, history does not relate.

Next as to the etymology of Piquet.

"The new World of Words" collected and published by E. P.[hillips]," (London. Ed. 1696.), states that Piquet is "perhaps so called as a diminutive of Pique, as it were a small Contest or Combat." The first edition is dated 1658; but Piquet does not occur in it, nor in the editions of 1662 and 1671.

Skeat ("Etymological Dictionary." Oxford.

1882.), remarks on E. P.'s proposed derivation, "This is ingenious and perhaps true."

According to the Abbé Bullet ("*Recherches sur les Cartes à jouer.*" Lyon. 1757.), the word Piquet is derived from Celtic. *Piquo*, he says, in Celtic signifies to choose, and *pic* and *repic* (the old spelling of pique and repique), have the sense of doubled and redoubled. The old spelling of pique was *picq* and of repique *repicq*, but that is a trifle. The ancient name of the point, *ronfle*, Bullet compounds of two Celtic words—*rum*, a gathering together, and *bell* (in composition, *fell*), a combat; hence *rumfell*, *rumfle*, *ronfle*, an assemblage of cards of the same suit.

"Pick" probably does belong to the Celtic languages, but there is no consequent reason for associating it with the game of Piquet. Skeat says of Celtic, "This is a particularly slippery subject to deal with," and "we must take care not to multiply the number [of borrowed Celtic words] unduly." Prior to the appearance of his "*Recherches,*" the Abbé was engaged on a Celtic dictionary, and he refers many words of doubtful etymology to Celtic. The coincidences he points out are generally regarded as more curious than valuable.

Grosley's fable that the game was invented by a man named Picquet would hardly be worth notice, but that it has been repeated (guardedly, it is true), by others. Persius says, "It appears very probable that this game bears the name of its inventor." And Littré has, "The game is supposed to have been named after its inventor."

It has already been pointed out that games like Piquet are not invented by any one person.

In the absence of a better etymology, the suggestion that the name of the game may have been derived from the spade suit, is submitted for consideration.

In the oldest known playing cards, combined with tarots, the suit of spades was represented by *bonâ fide* swords, and was named *spade* in Italian, *espadas* in Spanish. The sword also obtained, as a suit mark, in cards used in Germany; but the Germans soon altered it into *laub* or *grün*, the mark being shaped like a plum-leaf.

In numeral cards, unconnected with tarots, the suit of spades was called *picche* in Italian, *picas* in Spanish, as early as the time of Charles VII. of France.

The French appear to have adopted the German symbol, *grün*, and to have called it *pique*, after the Italian name. Leber, in a sentence translated by Chatto, says, "'In the southern parts of Europe the French *Pique* is *La Picca* or *La Spada*.'"

Merlin asserts that a game was played in Germany with sword cards, which in their composition resemble piquet packs; and conjectures that the French *Piquet* was analogous to this nameless game.

The suggestion, offered with hesitation, is that Piquet may be a developed form of the analogous

German game, and that, being played with *pique* cards in France, it may there consequently have obtained the name of *Piquet*.

Neither Cent nor Piquet are mentioned by Shakespeare. And it is somewhat remarkable that though Cent frequently occurs in English books of the Shakespearian period, Piquet, so far as is known, never does. In Nares' ("Glossary of Words in Works of English Authors of the Time of Shakespeare"), Cent and many other games find a place, but Piquet does not appear. From this it may be concluded that Cent was played in England until about the middle of the seventeenth century, when the word Cent went out of use, and was replaced by the word Piquet.

That the two games were practically identical will presently be made evident. The change from Cent to Piquet, in England, may therefore be regarded as one of name only, and may perhaps be thus accounted for. From the time of the marriage of Mary with Philip of Spain (1554), the English equivalent of the Spanish name of the game was in vogue. In 1625, Charles I. married the daughter of Henry IV. of France. When a French Princess came on the scene the French name, Piquet, was contemporaneously substituted for the Spanish name.

Cent was sometimes corrupted into Saunt, Saint, Cente, Sent, and Sant; and the word occasionally has the prefix "Mount." So far as is known, the meaning of this prefix has never been explained. A few quotations from authors of the period (1532 to 1656), may prove of interest.

The earliest known reference to Cent is in "A Manifest Detection of the most vyle and detestable Use of Diceplay, and other Practises lyke the same; A Myrour very necessary for all younge Gentilman and others sodenly enabled by worldly Abûdance, to loke in. Newly set forth for theire Behoufe.", a very rare tract, printed in 1532, and said to be by Gilbert Walker. The Percy Society's reprint (1850.), is quoted:—

"'After the table was removed, in came one of the waiters with a fair silver bowl, full of dice and cards. * * * Then each man choose his game.'"

The writer goes on to say, "'Because I alleged ignorance [of dice] * * * we fell to Saunt, five games a crown.'" This looks as though the stake was on the old-fashioned *partie*, best of five games.

Another early reference is to be met with in Turberville's "Book of Faulconrie" (1575.):—

"At coses or at Saunt to sit,
Or set their rest at prime."

In the "Book of Howshold Charges and other Paiments laid out by the L.[ord] North and his Commandement" (Nichol's "Progresses of Queen Elizabeth"), there are several entries of losses at play. In the entry, 1578, May 15 to 17, there occurs, "Lost at Saint, xv.s."

This is interesting, as showing that at that time Cent was a fashionable game, and played at court. Lord North used frequently to play with the Queen, and there are several entries of money lost to her, but the names of the games are omitted.

Northbrooke calls the game Cente. In "A Treatise, wherein Dicing, Daûcing, Vaine Plaies or Enterludes are reprooved". (London. 1577.), the author thus addresses the reader :—

"What is a man now a daies if he knows not fashions? * * * To plaie their twentie, fortie, or 100.*l.* at Cardes, Dice, &c., Post, Cente, Gleke or such other games : if he cannot thus do he is called a miser, a wretch, a lobbe, a cloune, and one that knoweth no fellowship nor fashions, and less honestie."

The "honestie" is not apparent in all cases. In "No-body and Some-body", an anonymous play (*circa* 1592.), Lord Sicophant confers with Somebody, the stage villain, as to introducing "Deceitfull Cards" at Court, the guilt to be made to rest with No-body. During the conversation, Sicophant shows cards prepared for cheating at various games, and, (*l.* 1533), says, "These are for saunt."

This is no mere effort of imagination on the part of the playwright. The use of "Deceitfull Cards" at Saunt, about this time, was unfortunately a fact. They are mentioned in "Dice Play"; and the action of Baxter *vers.* Woodyard and others", brought in 1605, was for cheating at this game with prepared cards, as the following extract from Moore's "Reports" (1688.) shows:—

"*Accoñ sur le case sur deceit enter eux practise p̄ luy disceaver al Cards, al un game le Mountsant, per inducer d'un Carde appel le Bumcarde per que ils devise que le pl'* [plaintiff] *n' averoit que tiels games que ils pleront, & joyndront ascun foits à lour pleasure, per quel cosonage & deceite,* colore ludendi, *ils defraud le pl' de* 16*l. les def. pleade* non culp', *& le Jury eux trove culp' & assesse damages.*"

In Minsheu's "Pleasant and delightfull Dialogues, Spanish and English" (London. 1599.), the game is also called Mount Sant. In the third Dialogue between "five gentlemen friendes," Rodricke, Sir Lorenzo and Mendoza converse thus:—

"R. Here are the cards. What shall we play at?

* * * * * *

L. At Mount Sant.

M. It makes my head to be in a swoune to be alwaies counting."

In "A Woman kilde with Kindnesse," a play, by Thomas Heywood, acted before the year 1604, Cent is called Saint: "Husband, shall we play at Saint?" and in Gervas Markham's "Famous —— or Noble Curtezan" (1609.), Cent is called Mount-cent:—

"Were it Mount-cent, primero, or at chesse,
    I wan with most, and lost still with the lesse."

Brewer ("Lingua, or the Combat of the Tongue and five Senses." 1607.), reverts to the older spelling Saunt. "As for Memory, he's a false hearted fellow, he always deceives them; they respect not him, except it be to play a Game at Chests, Primero, Saunt, Maw, or such like."

In "The Dumb Knight" (1608.), by Lewis Machin, there is a direct statement that the name of the game was derived from a hundred. The play also contains, in punning allusions to the love affairs of two of the characters, important materials for establishing the great similarity of Cent to Piquet.

"Enter aloft to cards the Queen and Phyloclcs.

Q. Come, my Lord, take your place, here are cards, and here are my crowns.

P. And here are mine; at what game will your Majesty play?

Q. At Mount-Saint.

P. A royal game, and worthy of the name
And meetest even for Saints to exercise;
Sure it was of a woman's first invention.

Q. It is not Saint, but Cent, taken from hundreds.

P. True, for 'mongst millions hardly is found one saint.

Q. Indeed you may allow a double game.
But come, lift for the dealing: it is my chance to deal.

P. An action most, most proper to your sex.

* * * * * *

Q. What are you, my Lord?

P. Your Highness' servant, but misfortune's slave.

Q. Your game, I mean.

P. Nothing in show, yet somewhat in account:
Madam, I am blank.

Q. You are a double game, and I am no less.
There's an hundred, and all cards made but one knave.

* * * * * *

What's your game now?
P. Four king's, as I imagine.
Q. Nay, I have two, yet one doth me little good.
P. Indeed, mine are two queens, and one I'll throw away.

* * * * * *

P. Can you decard, madam?
Q. Hardly, but I must do hurt."

Here the mention of showing, of the blank (carte blanche), of double games (counted in the old fashioned partie), of four kings, of throwing away, and of the decard (discard) prove conclusively the likeness of the two games.

In Taylor's "Motto" (1621.), Cent, under the spelling Sant, is enumerated among the games at which the prodigal "flings his money free with carelessnesse":—

"Ruffe, Slam, Trump, Nody, Whisk, Hole, Sant, New Cut."

In the "Annalia Dubrensia. Upon the yerely celebration of Mr. Robert Dover's Olimpick games upon Cotswold Hills" (1636.), a very rare book of which a copy is preserved in the Grenville Library, contributed to by thirty-two authors of the period, including Michael Drayton, Ben Jonson, Trussell, and others of less note, the game is spelt Cent. In the eulogium on Dover by William Denny this passage occurs:—

"Cent for those Gentry, who their states have marr'd,
That Game befitts them, for they must discard."

This again shows that discarding was part of the game.

Sir William Davenant, Poet Laureate after Ben Jonson, in "The Witts, a Comedy present'd at the Private House in Black Fryers" (1636.), spells the game Sent:—

"While their glad sons are left seven for their chance
At hazard: hundred and all made at Sent."

The inference is, as before, that "Sent" was played a hundred up.

The following quotation from "The Discovery of a most Exquisite Jewel, found in the Kennel of Worcester Streets, the Day after the Fight" (1651.), by Sir Thomas Urquhart of Cromarty, shows that the name of the game was sometimes anglicised into Hundred: "Verily I think they make use of Kings as we do of card Kings in playing at the Hundred; any one whereof, if there be appearance of a better game without him (and that the exchange of him for another incoming card is likely to conduce more for drawing the stake), is by good gamesters without any ceremony discarded."

If further evidence is required that the game of Cent was so called from its being played a hundred up, it may be obtained from a little book, published in 1656, entitled "The Scholer's Practicall Cards," by F. Jackson, M.A. It is chiefly occupied with instructions how to spell, write, cypher, and cast accounts, by means of cards. Several games are mentioned in it, and among them Saunt which the author explains by *centum*, a hundred.

Probably the earliest mention of Piquet, in print, is by Rabelais (1535). As already stated, he includes it in the list of games played by Gargantua; and it is to be noted that *le Cent* and *la Ronfle* are also to be found there.

It is not until after the lapse of rather more than a hundred years that Piquet appears with any frequency in French books, or at all in English books. It will be convenient first to take a few of the most interesting French references of the seventeenth century, and then to review Piquet in England from that time to the present.

The earliest work on Piquet extant is, probably, "*Le Royal Ieu dv Piqvet plaisant & recreatif. Reueu et corrigé en cette derniere Édition, pour le Contentement de ceux qui font Profession d'en observer les Règles.*" (*Rouen.* 1647.). This is the earliest edition to be met with in the British Museum. The book was translated into English in 1651, with the following title:—"The Royall and delightfull game of Picquet written in French and now rendred into English out of the last French edition. London. Printed for J. Martin and J. Ridley, and are to be sold at the Castle in Fleet-street nere Ram alley."

The following is the translation of the preface:—

"There comming to my hands, not long since, a small Treatise, concerning the game of PICQUET, and having perused the same; I have since thought fit to communicate it to the World; as being a game approved of everywhere, especially among the Gentry, and persons of Honour. It is a kind of Divertion, so sweet, and pleasing, as that it makes the houres slide away insensibly: it easeth the Gouty person; cleares up the melancholicke spirit; and refresheth the pensive Lover. These considerations are of sufficient force to put in any one a desire to the Play: But that which should most stir you up to the purchasing of this Booke, is, that you have here laid downe before you, an absolute, and exact account of the whole Game, and have all the difficulties, that may arise therein, fully resolved. If you therefore but observe the Rules and Maximes here delivered; you shall avoid all the quarrells, which usually arise amongst Gamesters, for want of being thoroughly informed in the Game; and shall preserve mutuall Society, which is the Bond that unites all things. Be sure, therefore, that you purchase this Booke: For in so doing, you shall not only much advantage your selves, but me also."

According to this treatise the game was played with thirty-six cards, the sixes remaining in the pack; the set or number up was a matter of agreement, but was usually fixed at a hundred, it being "in the choice of the Gamesters to make it more or lesse." In cutting for deal, more than one card must be "lifted," as the top one might be known by the back. In this remark is seen the reason for several of the severe rules which formerly obtained at Piquet, such, for instance, as allowing no change of discard after touching—

not looking at, but touching—the stock. In the days when cards were not so well manufactured as now, it is easy to understand that a pack might frequently contain marked cards, and, therefore, no one was allowed even to touch the stock without penalty.

In cutting for deal, "whichsoever of the two dips the least card" deals. The deal was either by two at a time, or by three or four at a time, to each player, at the option of the dealer; but he was bound to continue dealing through the game as he began, or, at least, to announce, before the cut, that he would change his method. The same object is apparent here as before, viz., that no advantage should be taken of a marked card. Twelve cards were given to each player, and twelve were left in the stock, of which the elder hand might take eight, the younger, four; each player being bound to discard one card. With thirty-six cards it was possible for both players to hold a *carte blanche*, and this case is provided for, the two annulling each other. The point was called the ruffe, in the French Treatise, *ronfle*. The description of the way of counting the point explains why points ending in a . four counted one less than the number of cards. The point was not formerly reckoned by cards but by tens (*dixaines*); and "For every Ten that he can reckon, he is to set up One. As, for example, for Thirty, he is to reckon Three, for Fourty, Foure: and so upward. Where, by the way, it is to be noted, that you are to reckon as much for Thirty five as for Forty; and as much for Forty five as for Fifty: and so of the rest: but for thirty six, thirty seven, Thirty eight, or Thirty nine, you are to reckon no more than for Thirty five: in like manner as for Thirty one, Thirty two, Thirty three or Thirty four, you are to reckon no more than for Thirty." When the game came to be played with thirty-two cards, points ending in a two or in a three could no longer be held, but those ending in a four could, and, the old method of reckoning being continued, it seemed as though a point ending in a four was an arbitrary exception to the rule of reckoning one for each card.

A curious expression is used in respect of the highest sequence making good all lower ones in the same hand, notwithstanding the adversary may hold intermediate ones. The best sequence is said to "drown" all the sequences held by the opponent. Cards under a ten did not reckon in play. It seems that in Paris it was permitted to amend incorrect calls of point or sequence, but not in Provence or Languedoc, where "the First word is alwaies to stand."

A few years later was published "*La Maison Académique*" (Paris. 1654.), in which appears "*Le Ieu du Picquet*" as then played. The general directions for play are almost identical with those in "*Le Royal Ieu du Piquet.*"

That Piquet was much played in France about this time is made evident by the publication of these books, by its repeated mention in Molière's plays, and by its having been chosen as the title of the ballet, already referred to.

"*Les Fâcheux*," by Molière (1661.), contains an interesting Piquet hand, which deserves more than a passing notice. The description, freely translated, runs thus:—

"Console me, Marquis, for the extraordinary partie at Piquet I lost yesterday against St. Bouvain, a man to whom I could deal and give fifteen points. It is a maddening coup which crushes me, and which makes me wish all players at the devil;—a coup enough to make a man go and hang himself. I only wanted two points; he required a pique. I dealt; he proposed a fresh deal. I, having pretty good cards in all suits, refused. He takes six cards. Now observe my bad luck: I carry ace of clubs; ace, king, knave, ten, eight of hearts; and throw out (as I considered it best to keep my point), king, queen of diamonds, and queen, ten of spades. I took in the queen to my point, which made me a quint major. To my amazement, my adversary showed the ace and a sixième minor in diamonds, the suit of which I had discarded king and queen. But, as he required a pique, I was not alarmed, expecting to make at least two points in play. In addition to his seven diamonds he had four spades, and, playing them, he put me to a card, for I did not know which of my aces to keep. I thought it best to throw the ace of hearts, but he had discarded all his four clubs, and capoted me with the six of hearts! I was so vexed I could not say a word. Confound it! why do I have such frightful luck?"

Supplying the unnamed cards, St. Bouvain's hand would be knave, ten, nine, eight, seven, six of diamonds; king, queen, nine, seven of clubs; and nine, seven of hearts. He discards the four clubs and the two hearts; he takes in ace of diamonds; six of hearts; and ace, king, knave, eight of spades.

Alcippe (his adversary), deals himself king, queen of diamonds; queen, ten of spades; ace, king, knave, ten, eight of hearts; and ace, knave, eight of clubs. He discards the diamonds, spades, and knave, eight of clubs; he takes in nine, seven, six of spades; queen of hearts; and ten, six of clubs.

St. Bouvain's point and sixième are good for twenty-three; he plays the diamonds and spades, which include six counting cards, making him twenty-nine; and there is one card to be played. Alcippe reckons nothing, and has to play eleven cards. He must keep either ace of hearts or ace of clubs. He elects to keep the club. St. Bouvain wins the last trick with the six of hearts (this is a non-counting card; but, if it wins, it reckons one for the last trick), and piques and capots his opponent.

Molière has skilfully heaped up the various small worries that may annoy an irritable player during a hand. The score is one source of annoyance :—St. Bouvain wants a pique, Alcippe only wants two points, and has such cards that, though a pique is not impossible it is in the highest degree improbable. As Fielding ("Tom Jones") truly remarks, "The gamester who loses a party at Piquet by a single point, laments his bad luck ten times as much as he who never came within a prospect of the game." Again, Alcippe has the chance offered him of a fresh deal, which implies that his adversary has very bad cards. The fresh deal is refused, and, notwithstanding, St. Bouvain wins. Then the elder hand, having a right to take eight cards, only takes six, which is a disagreeable surprise after proposing a fresh deal, as Alcippe would naturally wonder how it could be that, notwithstanding the bad hand, St. Bouvain can afford to leave two cards; and, lastly, Alcippe is put to a card, which is by no means pleasant at any time, but is most unpleasant of all to a player with two aces, who only requires one trick to win the partie, and who loses it if he keeps the wrong one.

Alcippe, though he boasts his superior play, and declares that he lost by bad luck, really makes two mistakes which lose him the game. First, he does not discard to the score. His game, when wanting to score only two, is to protect himself from a capot by throwing out his point. If he discards ace, knave, ten, eight of hearts, and knave, eight of clubs, he is morally certain to win. Next, he plays badly in throwing the ace of hearts. It is evident that, in order to save the game, St. Bouvain's last card must be a non-counting card. Now, he may hold any one of three non-counting hearts, or either of two non-counting clubs. This being so, it is three to two in favour of keeping the heart.

In 1676 was produced "*Le Triomphe des Dames,*" with the ballet interlude, about which so much has been written by Piquet historians. As it has often been stated that this play was never printed, it may be as well to give the title and publisher's name in full :—

"*Le Triomphe des Dames. Comédie mesléc d'Ornaments avec Explication ou Combat à la Barrière et de toutes les Devises, par Th.*[omas] *Corneille, représentée par la Trouppe du Roy. Étallie au Fourbourg S. Germain. Paris. Jean Ribon.* 1676."

The "*Théâtre François*" describes the ballet thus :—

"*En 1676, on représenta sur le Théâtre de l'Hotel Guénégaud une Comédie de Thomas Corneille, en cinq actes, intitulée le Triomphe des Dames, qui n'a point été imprimée, & dont le Ballet du Jeu de Piquet étoit un des Intermedes. * * * Les Rois, les Dames & les Valets, après avoir formé, par leurs danses, des tierces et des quatorzes; après s'être rangés, tous les noirs d'un côté, & les rouges de l'autre, finirent par un contre-danse, où toutes les couleurs étoient mêlées confusément, et sans suite.*"

"*La Maison Académique,*" after several editions, gave place to the more comprehensive "*Académie Universelle des Jeux.*" This work, variously edited and augmented, was the French authority on games for about a century and a half. The later editions are mainly reprints of the previous ones; and, probably owing to the book's not keeping pace with the times, it gradually lost its prestige. Modern "*Académies*" there are still; but they are no more like the older ones than modern "Hoyles" are like the "Short Treatises" of Hoyle.

The *Académies*, properly so called, nearly all agree on two points. They give Piquet the first or second place among card games; and they derive a good deal of their Piquet inspiration from "*Le Royal Jeu dv Piqvet.*"

The French *Académie* was translated into English about 1768. The title of the book is:—"The Academy of Play; Containing a full Description of; and the Laws of Play, Now observed in the several Academies of Paris, Relative to The following Games, viz. [Here follow the names of thirty-three card games.] From the French of the Abbé Bellecour. London: Printed for F. Newbery, the Corner of St. *Paul's Church-Yard, Ludgate-Street.*"

The preface says, "The Game of *Piquet* is * * * here treated in a manner more clear, and more conformable to the present Practice, as in all the Rules here given, we have followed the Determinations of the most able Players."

The "Determinations of the most able Players" enable the reader to trace the origin of the proverb that "Piquet is not a game of surprise," a saying not always true of the game. It refers to changing the suit when playing the cards:—

"You have to observe that as there is no advantage to be taken by surprize, at the Game of PIQUET he that in playing, changes his Suit, is to name the Suit in which he then leads; in default of which, the other Party, supposing that he still continues to lead in the former Suit, has a right to take up the Card that he has played, even tho' it should be in the Suit in which he then leads."

And this is the penalty, when "surprises" of a more serious nature are detected :—

"*Qui reprend des cartes dans son écart, est surpris à en changer, ou fait d'autres tours de fripon, perd la partie, et doit être chassé comme un coquin avec qui on ne doit plus jouer. La peine de cet article ne saurait être assez forte, puisque c'est pour punir un fripon avéré.*"

This is quaintly translated as follows :—

"He who takes in any part of his Discard, or is detected in changing his Cards, or in any other kind of fraud; loses the party, and ought to be drove out as a cheat; with whom no one ought to play.

The punishment here cannot be sufficiently severe, as it is intended to chastise a manifest scoundrel."

The only points of importance in which the Abbé's "Academy" differs from "The Royall and delightfull game of Picquet", (the same alterations being present in the corresponding French editions), are that thirty-two cards are substituted for thirty-six, and consequently that the number taken after discarding is five instead of eight elder hand, and three instead of four younger hand: that dealing by four cards at a time is no longer permitted; that the *ronfle* or ruffe is called the point; that sometimes every card of the point is allowed to reckon;

and that the counting in play of cards below a ten is optional.

The above changes in the mode of play were introduced about the end of the seventeenth century.

Piquet, according to popular belief, was imported into England from France.

> "Vat have you of *grand plaisir* in dis towne,
> Vidout it come from France, dat vill go down?
> Picquet, basset; your *vin*, your dress, your dance;
> 'Tis all you see, *tout à la mode de France.*"
> —FARQUHAR.
> Epilogue to "Sir Harry Wildair" (1701).

But, as has been seen, the game first came to this country as Cent; and there is nothing to show whether it was of French or of Spanish importation.

Be this as it may, Cent was deposed in England, in favour of Piquet, about the middle of the seventeenth century. One of the earliest writers to refer to Piquet under its new name is John Hall, in his "Horæ Vacivæ" (1646). He says:—"For Cardes, the Philologil of them is not for an essay; a man's fancy would be sum'd up at Cribbidge; Glecke requires a vigilant memory: Maw, a pregnant agility; Picket a various invention; Primero, a dexterous kinde of rashness."

In 1659, a curious pamphlet (now rare) was published, entitled,—"Shufling, *Cutting,* and *Deal-ing,* in A Game at Pickquet: being Acted from the

Year, 1653. to 1658. By *O. P.* [Oliver Protector] And others; With great Applause." It represents Cromwell, after the Long Parliament, playing cards with some old officers, friends, and opponents, the players expressing their political sentiments through allusions to the game of Piquet:—

"OLIVER P. I am like to have a good beginning on't: I have thrown out all my best Cards, and got none but a Company of Wretched ones; so I may very well be capetted [capoted]."

One of the characters says, "I am nothing but a Ruff" (*ronfle* or point). Another, "I got more the last Game when I plaid Cent: for I had a hundred, and all made."

A similar squib was published in "*Mélanges Historiques de Bois Jourdain*", some half century later. It alludes to the state of France on the accession of Louis XV. The following is a specimen:—

"LE JEU DE PIQUET, 1716. LES EXILÉS—*Un quatorze de roi* [Louis XIV.] *avait gâté notre jeu; une quinte de roi* [Louis XV.] *le rend plus beau.*"

In "The Wild Gallant" (1662.), Dryden's first acted play, there is drawn the singular picture of a man playing Piquet against an imaginary adversary, who however arrives in time to pick up the stakes:—

"A Table set with Cards upon it.

TRICE. * * * Ay, it shall be he: Jack Loveby, what think'st thou of a game at Piquet, we two hand to fist? You and I will play one single game for ten pieces: 'Tis deep stake, Jack, but 'tis all one between us two: You shall deal, Jack:—Who I, Mr. Justice? That's a good one; you must give me use for your hand then; that's six i' the hundred. [The advantage of the deal was formerly estimated at about seven points in a hundred.]—Come, lift, lift;—mine's a ten; Mr. Justice:—Mine's a king; oh, ho, Jack, you deal. I have the advantage of this, i' faith, if I can keep it. (*He deals twelve apiece, two by two, and looks on his own cards.*) I take seven, and look on this—Now for you, Jack Loveby.

Enter LOVEBY, *behind*.

Lov. How's this? Am I the man he fights with?

Trice. I'll do you right, Jack; As I am an honest man, you must discard this; There's no other way: If you were my own brother, I could do no better for you.—Zounds, the rogue has a quint-major, and three aces younger hand.—(*Looks on the other cards.*) Stay; What am I for the point? But bare forty, and he fifty-one: fifteen, and five for the point, twenty, and three by aces, twenty-three; Well, I am to play first: one, twenty-three; two, twenty-three; three, twenty-three; four, twenty-three; now I must play into his hand: five: now you take it, Jack;—five, twenty-four, twenty-five, twenty-six, twenty-seven, twenty-eight, twenty-nine, thirty and the cards forty.

Lov. [*aside*] Hitherto it goes well on my side.

Trice. Now I deal: How many do you take, Jack? All. Then I am gone: what a rise is here? Fourteen by aces, and a sixième-major; I am gone, without looking into my cards.—(*Takes up an ace and bites it.*) Ay, I thought so: If ever man play'd with such cursed fortune, I'll be hanged, and all for want of this damned ace.—There's your ten pieces, you rooking, beggarly rascal as you are.

LOVEBY *enters*.

Lov. What occasion have I given you for these words, Sir? Rook and Rascal! I am no more rascal than yourself, Sir!

Trice. How's this? How's this?

Lov. And though for this time I put it up because I am a winner—(*Snatches the gold.*)

Trice. What a devil dost thou put up? Not my gold, I hope, Jack?

Lov. By your favour, but I do; and 'twas won fairly: a sixième, and fourteen aces, by your own confession."

In " Flora's Vagaries," a comedy printed in 1670, Piquet is again introduced :—

"Grimani. Well, lay by your work, we will have a game at cards. Giacomo, go fetch some cards and counters, picket you play well at.

Otrante [his daughter]. I am no Gamester, but if you please to play—

*   *   *   *   *   *

Gri. Sit down, come, lift, I deal. How many take you in?

Otr. I take seven, Sir.

Gri. Take them and I will have all the rest. So now, what say you to the point?

Otr. A little game, some three-and-fifty.

Gri. 'Tis good, hunch out.

Otr. Quart major.

Gri. And that too.

*   *   *   *   *   *

Otr. Three kings.

Gri. No, that's not good.

Otr. Nine, and there's ten, eleven, twelve, thirteen.

Gri. I had forgot my aces.

*   *   *   *   *   *

Otr. You have lost you aces, fourteen."

The action of the play then causes the game to stop.

It is interesting to observe that the score was marked with counters, and that the mode of play was as now, except that the pack was composed of thirty-six cards, otherwise Otrante could not take seven cards, and could not have a point of fifty-three, as with a thirty-two card pack this point cannot be made. (*See* pp. 63–65, for an account of the old mode of playing.)

The occurrence of Piquet in dramatic and other writings of this period is very common.

About this time appeared, "Wit's Interpreter: the English Parnassus." The third edition, with many additions, by "J. C.", is dated 1671. One part containing "Games and Sports now us'd at this day among the Gentry of England, &c.", has instructions for playing "The Ingenious Game called Picket." Picket is also included among the card games in Cotton's "Compleat Gamester" (1674). In both cases "The Royall and delightfull game of Picquet" has been plagiarised. In the edition of "The Compleat Gamester" of 1709 a note is added, that "These were the Rules of the Game when it was play'd with the sixes, but however the Rules hold for the Game as it is play'd at present without the Sixes, only when it is play'd without the Sixes the Elder Hand is to take Five of the Eight Cards in the Stock." This fixes the time when the alteration of the pack became generally recognised in England.

At the beginning of the eighteenth century, card-playing was the rage in all parts of Europe. The games most in favour, with people of fashion in England, were Ombre, Piquet and Basset (now called Faro). In "The Confederacy" by

Vanbrugh (1705), Clarissa exclaims, "We'll play at Ombre, Piquet, Basset, and so forth, and close the evening with a handsome supper and ball." Other games are referred to, but not so frequently. In "Sir Harry Wildair," (1701), for example, the following conversation occurs:—

"SIR HARRY. The capot at Piquet, the paroli at Basset, and then Ombre! Who can resist the charms of Matadores?

LADY LUREWELL. Ay, Sir Harry; and then the *sept le va! Quinze le va! Trente le va!* [Basset].

SIR H. Right, right, Madam!

LADY LURE. Then the nine of diamonds at Comet [Pope Joan], three fives at Cribbage, and Pam [Knave of Clubs] in Lanterloo [Loo], Sir Harry!

SIR H. Ay, Madam, these are charms indeed. Then the pleasure of picking your husband's pocket over night to play at Basset next day."

About this date Piquet is sometimes spelt Piquette, as though the idea had gained ground that the word is a diminutive of *pique* (*see* p. 52). The first volume of Thomas D'Urfey's celebrated poems, "Wit and Mirth: or Pills to purge Melancholy," (1719.), contains "A Poole at Piquette, The Words made and set to a Tune, by Mr. D'Urfey, made at Ramsbury Mannor."

> "Within an Arbour of delight,
>   As sweet as Bowers Elisian
> Where famous *Sidney* us'd to write
>   I lately had a Vision:
> Methought beneath a Golden State,
>   The Turns of Chance obeying,
> Six of the World's most noted great,
>   At *Piquette* were a playing.

"The first two were the brave *Eugene*
  With *Vendosme* Battle waging;
The next a Nymph who to be Queen,
  Her *Mounsieur* was Engaging;
The *Fleur de Lis* Old *Maintenon*
  With sanctified *Carero*;
And next above the scarlet *Don*,
  Queen ANNE, and *Gallick Nero*.

"The Game between the Martial braves,
  Was held in diff'rent Cases;
The French man got Quatorze of Knaves,
  But Prince *Eugene* four Aces:
And tho' the 'tothers eldest Hand
  Gave Hopes to make a Jest on't,
Yet now the Point who soonest gain'd
  Could only get the best on't.

"From them I turned mine Eyes to see
  The Church man and the Lady,
And found her pleas'd to high degree
  Her Fortune had been steady,
The Saints that cram'd the *Spanish* Purse
  She hop'd would all oblige her,
For he had but a little *Terse*
  When she produc'd *Quint-Major*.

"And now betwixt the *King* and *Queen*
  An Empire was depending;
Within whose mighty Game was seen
  The Art of State-contending:
The *Mounsieur* had three Kings to win't
  And was o'er *Europe* roaming,
But her full Point *Quatorze* and *Quint*
  Won all and left him foaming."

Again, in Pope's "Moral Essays in four Epistles," (1733.), in the first of which the character of Lord Godolphin is sketched, it is stated that

"His pride is in Piquette,
Newmarket fame, and judgment in a bet."

In 1719 Richard Seymour published "The Court Gamester: or full and easy Instructions for * * * Ombre, Picquet, and the Royal Game of Chess." Much of the Piquet is derived from the original source; but there are considerable additions, and quaint remarks peculiar to this treatise which deserve quotation. Speaking of tierces and other sequences, Seymour observes, "These Terms may sound a little like conjuring, to Persons that don't understand them; but they are only the *French* Terms that we make use of, because we have not *English* whereby to express the same thing in one Word." Further on, after explaining the annulling of minor sequences by major ones, he adds, "Thus, among Cards as well as Men, the Great still overcome the Small."

The directions are repeated in seven editions up to 1750; in the fifth edition it is stated that "Piquet is now become so common that even the meanest people have become instructed, and let into all the Tricks and Secrets of it." This, however, is doubtful, for though Piquet was much played in the clubs, and in fashionable society, in the middle of the eighteenth century, it never appears, in this country, to have been the game of the masses, as it is in France.

Àpropos of club play, about this time, a story is told in Walpole's "Letters" of Selwyn's walking into White's, in November, 1752, where he found James Jeffries playing Piquet with Sir Edward Falkener, who was at that time Joint Postmaster-

General. "Oh," quoth Selwyn, "he is now robbing the mail!"

The "Court Gamester" was eventually amalgamated with the "Compleat Gamester"; and, in the eighth edition (1754) a number of Hoyle's rules and cases are plagiarised.

Bath was the head quarters of fashionable card-playing about the middle of the eighteenth century. It is related of a notorious gambler, named Lookup, that he won large sums of money of Lord Chesterfield, chiefly at Piquet, and that, with his winnings, he built some houses at Bath, which he jocularly called "Chesterfield Row." Lookup died in 1770, with cards in his hand, while playing the game of humbug, or two-handed whist. Foote, on hearing this, said, "Lookup is humbugged out of the world at last."

The Bath play continued until about the year 1840, a *coterie* of distinguished Piquet players constantly meeting there during the early part of the present century; and the club play continued at White's and Graham's. When the Bath play declined, and Graham's club was broken up, Piquet pretty well died out in England, almost the only place where it was regularly played being the Portland Club. Recently Piquet has revived; and it is now (1890) so much played in England, that it may be called a popular game.

The last work on the game which calls for notice here is Hoyle's "Short Treatise on the Game of Piquet." (1744.) This is original, and not, like the others, taken from the older books. Though somewhat obscure in style, it contains much valuable instruction, and also the laws of the game, which were the only authority in this country until the code of the Portland Club was published in 1873. Hoyle's laws were twenty-six in number, and were all observed by strict players. Editors of Hoyle, however, subsequent to 1800, took the liberty of adding nine other laws on their own account. These added laws had no weight, and, in several instances, the practice of club players was opposed to them.

Hoyle does not fix the number the game is to be played up, probably because it was still a matter of agreement in his day. His editors, however, in copies published after Hoyle's death, say the game is a hundred-and-one up. *Piquet au cent* is played a hundred-and-one up in some parts of France at the present day (1873); but the practice in this country, and in Paris when Piquet *au cent* is played, is to make the game a hundred up. Piquet *au cent* is now (1885), however, almost entirely superseded by the Rubicon Game. The introduction of this form of Piquet necessitated the redrawing of the Portland code. In this task the Turf Club assisted; and, since 1882, the joint code of these two clubs has ruled the game among English players.

It is somewhat remarkable that so fine a game as Piquet should have been almost entirely neglected by writers on games from 1744 to 1873

G

(nearly a hundred-and-thirty years), except by editors of Hoyle. This is the more singular, as it is generally admitted that Hoyle's laws and directions for play, though excellent as far as they go, are by no means complete. In the following pages an attempt has been made to supplement Hoyle's work, by giving a full description of the modern game (Piquet *au cent* being now seldom played), and by enlarging more thoroughly on the various points of play.

DESCRIPTION OF THE GAME.

INTRODUCTORY.

The Game of Piquet is played by two persons, with a pack of thirty-two cards—the sixes, fives, fours, threes, and twos, being thrown out from a complete pack. It is convenient to have two packs, each being used alternately.

DEALING.

The players cut for deal. The highest has choice. The order of the cards, both in cutting, and in calling and playing, is ace (highest), king, queen, knave, ten, nine, eight, seven (lowest).

The pack is then cut by the non-dealer, or *elder hand*, to the dealer, or *younger hand*, who re-unites the packets and gives the top two cards to his adversary, the next two to himself, and so on, dealing two cards at a time to each player, until they have twelve cards a-piece. Or, the deal may be by three at a time. The dealer places the undealt cards (called the *stock*), eight in number, face downwards on the table between the players. (*See* also Laws 1–17, pp. 1–3.)

DISCARDING.

The players then look at their hands and proceed to *discard*, *i.e.*, to put out such cards as they deem advisable (but *see* carte blanche, p. 95). They then take in an equivalent number of cards from the stock. The elder hand has the privilege of thus exchanging five of his cards. He may take any less number, but he must exchange one. He separates his discard from his hand, places it aside, face downwards on the table, and takes from the top of the stock the number of cards discarded.

If the elder hand takes all his five cards he leaves three for the younger hand. If he discards less than five cards (leaving more than three in the stock) he announces the fact by saying, "I only take four,"—or three, or less, as the case may be; or, "I leave a card,"—or two, or more cards, as the case may be.

When the elder hand discards less than five cards he is entitled to look at the cards he leaves. For example: If he discards four cards, he takes the top four cards of the stock, and looks at the fifth, the one left on the top of the stock after he has taken his four. If he discards but three cards, he may similarly look at the two cards left, and so on. He returns the cards thus looked at to the top of the stock without showing them to his adversary.

The younger hand has the privilege of discarding three cards. He is obliged to discard one.

If the elder hand has left any of his cards, the younger hand may take all that remain in the stock, discarding an equal number. Thus, if the elder hand has left one card, the younger may take four, viz., the one left and his own three. He separates his discard from his hand, and lays it aside as explained in respect of the elder hand; and, in a similar way, takes his cards from the stock after the elder hand has taken in.

Whether the elder hand takes all his cards or not, the younger hand must take his cards from the top of the stock, including any card or cards that may have been left by the elder hand. For instance, the elder hand takes four cards; the younger hand only takes two, and leaves two cards. He must take the card left by the elder hand and the top card of the other three, and must leave the bottom two.

If the younger hand leaves any cards, he announces the number left. He has a right to look at cards he leaves, at any time before he plays to the first trick, but not afterwards. He must declare whether he will look at them or not as soon as the elder hand has named the suit he will first lead (which he generally does by leading a card). If the younger hand looks at them, or at any of them, he must also show all that are left to the elder hand, the elder hand first naming the suit he will lead. If the younger hand elects not to look at the cards left, the elder cannot see them.

Cards left untaken, and not looked at, must be kept separate from the hands and discards.

Each player may look at his own discard at any time during the play of the hand; but he must keep his discard separate from his other cards. (*See* also Laws 21–45, pp. 4–8.)

CALLING AND SHOWING.

The discarding and taking in being over, the players next announce or *call* certain combinations of the cards in hand, and, if *good*, score for them. These combinations are point, sequences, and quatorzes and trios.

The point must be announced first (Law 46). It is scored by the player who calls the suit of greatest number. If each player's best suit contains an equal number of cards, the point is then scored by the one who calls the suit of greatest strength, according to the following way of valuing it :—The ace is valued at eleven, each of the court cards at ten a-piece, and the other cards at the number of pips on each.

The elder hand calls his *point*, thus :—Suppose his best suit to consist of five cards. He would call, "Five cards." If the younger hand has no suit of equal or greater number, he replies, "Good." The elder hand then names the suit, saying, "In spades," or as the case may be, and counts one for each card, saying, "Five."

If the point called by the elder hand happens to be equal in number to the best suit of his adversary, the younger hand says, "Equal." The elder then announces the value of his cards. Thus :—The elder's point is ace, king, knave, nine, eight ; he would say, "Forty-eight," or,

"Making eight." If the younger hand's five cards make less than forty-eight, he replies, "Good," and the elder then names the suit. If the younger hand's point makes exactly forty-eight, he says, "Equal." The elder hand then names the suit in which his equality is, but does not count anything for it.

If the younger hand's five cards make more than forty-eight, he says, "Not good," and the elder hand does not name the suit he called.

If the younger hand has a point consisting of a greater number of cards than the one called by his adversary, he says, "Not good," and the elder does not name the suit he called.

When the younger hand's point is equal, he names the suit after the elder has finished calling his hand and has led a card, but he does not count anything for point. If the younger hand's point is good, he names the suit and reckons one for each card of the point as soon as the elder has led a card.

A player calling a point which is smaller than his best suit, can correct his miscall before the younger hand has answered, "Not good," or, "Equal."

It is usual, but not compulsory, to call sequences next after point; quatorze or trio may be called before sequence, without prejudice to a subsequent call of sequence.

The elder hand should first call his best *sequence*. Any three or more cards of the same suit held in hand in the order given at p. 83 constitute a sequence. Sequences, and the amounts reckoned for them when good, are as under:—

A sequence of eight cards (named a huitième) scores eighteen.
,,   seven   ,, (,,   septième)   ,,   seventeen.
,,   six   ,, (,,   sixième)   ,,   sixteen.
,,   five   ,, (,,   quint   )   ,,   fifteen.
,,   four   ,, (,,   quart   )   ,,   four.
,,   three   ,, (,,   tierce   )   ,,   three.

It will be observed that tierces and quarts reckon one for each card; and that higher sequences reckon one for each card, with ten added.

Sequences are further defined by name according to the card which heads them. Thus, a sequence of king, queen, knave, is named a tierce to a king; ace, king, queen, is called a tierce major; and so on for other sequences headed by an ace. A sequence of nine, eight, seven, is called a tierce minor; and so on for other sequences of the lowest cards.

Whether or not a sequence is good is determined by (*a*) the number of cards it contains, and by (*b*) the highness of the cards. A higher sequence is superior to or good against a lower one containing the same number of cards; but a sequence containing a greater number of cards, even though low ones, is good against a higher sequence containing fewer cards. For example:—
A tierce major is good against any other tierce; a quart minor is good against a tierce major.

The elder hand, when calling his sequence, names it thus :—"A quint minor," "A quart to a queen," or whatever it may be. The younger hand says, "Good," "Equal," or "Not good," as in the case of the point. If good or equal, the elder hand then names the suit in which his sequence is. If not good, the younger calls his sequence, and names the suit in which it is, after the elder has finished calling and has led a card.

When a player has a sequence that is good, he reckons one for each card of it, and an additional ten if it is a sequence of five or more cards (*see* p. 88). The player whose sequence is allowed to be good, is also entitled to reckon all smaller sequences in his hand, notwithstanding that his adversary holds a sequence of intermediate value. For example :—A has a quart to a queen (queen, knave, ten, nine) in one suit and a tierce minor (nine, eight, seven) in another suit; B has a quart to a knave (knave, ten, nine, eight) in a third suit. A calls a quart to a queen, which is good. He scores four for it, and then calls the tierce minor, and scores three for that. B's quart to a ten counts nothing, and does not prevent A from reckoning the tierce minor.

If the two players' sequences are equal, the equality is called by both, and neither scores anything for sequence, even though one player may hold a second sequence of equal value, or an inferior sequence. The equality of the superior sequence nullifies the whole. Thus:—A calls a tierce major; B says, "Equal." A and B are precluded from scoring a second tierce major or any smaller sequence.

If the elder hand inadvertently calls a low sequence, holding a higher one, he may correct his miscall before it has been replied to by the younger hand. After the younger hand has replied, "Good," or "Equal," the elder must abide by his call, and can only reckon sequences equal to, or lower than, the one he called. Thus:— A has a quart minor and a tierce minor. If he first calls a tierce minor, and it is admitted to be good, he can reckon two tierce minors, but he cannot reckon the quart.

There is one exception to this. If the elder hand calls a sequence that is *good against the cards* (*i.e.*, better than any sequence the younger hand could possibly have in hand and discard taken together), he can reckon any sequence he holds, even though it is better than the one first called. For example:—A has a quart to a king, and a tierce to a queen, good against the cards. If he first calls a tierce to a queen, he may afterwards reckon his quart.

Some players show all that they claim as good or equal; this, however, is not compulsory, unless the cards are asked for.

As the law now stands, calling is equivalent to showing. Hence, if A calls, say, "Forty-eight in diamonds," the only diamonds he can hold being ace, knave, ten, nine, eight, B is deemed to know that A holds a quart. A forgets to reckon his quart, and leads a card. B cannot reckon any equal or inferior sequence. If A remembers he has not reckoned the quart, he can rectify the omission before B has played to the first trick. (*See* Law 56, p. 11, and Case IV., p. 22.)

The younger hand is not bound to call his best sequence first. Thus, if the elder has called a tierce major, and the younger has replied, "Not good," the younger is at liberty to show and count a tierce minor first, and then a quart or larger sequence. The reason for the difference between the elder and younger hands in this respect is that the younger is only reckoning (adding up his score); but the elder is ascertaining whether what he calls is good, and, by calling a lower sequence before a higher, he might gain information as to the contents of his opponent's hand to which he is not entitled. The elder hand, however, having called a sequence which is good, may reckon lower sequences in any order for the same reason, viz., that he is then only adding up his score.

After sequence (but *see* p. 87), *quatorzes* (*i.e.*, four aces, kings, queens, knaves, or tens), or *trios* (three of any of these), are called and reckoned as before, except that in this combination there can be no equality. Quatorzes or trios of cards smaller than tens are of no value. A quatorze if good reckons fourteen (one for each card with ten added); a trio if good counts three. Any quatorze is good against a trio; thus, four tens are good against three aces. If each player has a quatorze the highest is good; the same if each has a trio; and, as in the case of sequences, anything that is good enables the player to count all smaller combinations of four or three in his hand, and nullifies any that the adversary may hold of intermediate value. For example:—A has four tens and three knaves; B, three aces. A scores fourteen for tens, and three for knaves; and B does not count his aces.

A quatorze or trio is called thus:—"Four aces," "Three queens," or as the case may be. The younger hand then says, "Good," or "Not good," as before. The cards of a quatorze or trio are never shown on the table. The adversary, however, has a right to demand their production if he thinks fit.

The reason that quatorzes are not shown is that when aces, kings, queens, knaves, or tens are called, the adversary knows what the cards are. When a player might hold a quatorze, but only calls three of that rank (as, *e.g.*, A calls three kings, when he might have held four), the adversary is entitled to know which card is not reckoned. In the case of the example given, B might say, "Show your kings," by which means he would ascertain the king that is not called. But the usual course is for B to say, "Which king do you not reckon?", and A is bound to reply.

PIQUET.

In calling quatorzes or trios the elder hand should call his best first, as, if he calls a lower one, he cannot afterwards reckon a higher one, unless the lower one is good against the cards. If the one first called is good, any lower ones may be reckoned without regard to order, as in the case of sequences.

The younger hand may reckon his quatorzes or trios, if good, in any order. He is not obliged first to call his best, and he may rectify a miscall of any kind until he has played to the first trick, for the reason already given (*see* p. 91).

After the elder hand has finished calling, and has reckoned all that he has good, he leads a card. Before playing to this card, the younger hand reckons all that he has good, or calls all that he has equal.

A player is not bound to call anything unless he pleases; and he may always call less than he holds, if he does not desire to expose his hand. (*See* also Laws 46–56, pp. 8–11.)

PLAYING.

The players having called what they have good or equal, and reckoned what they have good, next proceed to play the hands. The elder hand leads any card he pleases, and his opponent plays to it. The younger hand must follow suit if able, but otherwise he may play any card he thinks fit.

Two cards, one played by each player, constitute a *trick*. The trick is won by the player who plays to it the higher card of the suit led. A player is not obliged to win the card led unless he chooses, if he can follow suit without. The winner of the trick leads to the next, and so on, until all the twelve cards in each hand are played out.

During the play the leader counts one for each card led. He counts one whether he wins the trick or not. If the leader wins the trick, his adversary counts nothing in play; but if the second player wins the trick, he also counts one. The winner of the trick again counts one for the card he next leads, and so on.

The winner of the *last trick* counts two instead of one.

The tricks are left face upwards on the table in front of the player who wins them. They may be examined by either player at any time.

If each player wins six tricks, the cards are *divided*, and there is no further score. If one player wins more than six tricks (called winning *the cards*), he adds ten to his score, beyond what he has counted in hand and play. If one player wins every trick (called winning a *capot*), he adds forty to his score instead of ten, ten for the cards, and thirty for the capot.

All cards scored for as good, or called as equal, must be exhibited to the adversary if demanded during the play of the hand. This, however, does not apply to a call of an equal *number* of cards for point by the younger hand, when the *strength* of his point is inferior to that of the elder's. Among players, the cards are not as a rule exhibited; but all necessary questions with regard to them are replied to. Thus, A scores a point of five cards, and plays three of them. Presently, B wants to refresh his memory, so he says, " How many of your point have you?", or " How many spades?", or as the case may be; and A is bound to reply, " Two." Similarly, if A had scored three kings, B is entitled to a reply to the question, "What kings have you in hand?", or B might ask, " Have you anything in hand that you have called?", when A must tell him. (*See* also Laws 57-60, pp. 11, 12.)

CARTE BLANCHE, PIQUE AND REPIQUE.

In the foregoing pages carte blanche, pique and repique have been omitted in order to simplify the description of the game.

If either player has dealt to him a hand which contains neither king, queen, nor knave, he holds *carte blanche*. This entitles him to score ten. Before he takes in he must show the carte blanche by dealing his cards quickly one on top of the other, face upwards on the table, after which he retakes them into his hand. If either player has carte blanche, he must inform his adversary at once, by saying, " I have a carte blanche," or

"Discard for carte blanche." As soon as the adversary has discarded, the carte blanche is shown him. (*See* also Laws 18-20, pp. 3, 4.)

If the elder hand scores, *in hand and play*, thirty or more before his adversary counts anything that hand, he wins a *pique*. A pique entitles the player to add thirty to his score; but in all other respects the hand is played as already explained. For example:—A has a quint major, which is good for point and sequence, and three aces, which are also good. He counts twenty for the point and quint, and three for the aces, and then leads the quint major and the two aces, or one of the aces and some other card. This makes him thirty; and, as his adversary has not scored anything, it is a pique. A, when he leads the card which makes him thirty, instead of counting "Thirty," counts "Sixty." It is not necessary that the card led which makes thirty should win the trick. The elder hand, having reckoned twenty-nine when his adversary has reckoned nothing, and having the lead, wins a pique even if he leads a losing card.

If a player scores, *in hand alone*, thirty points or more by scores that reckon in order before anything that his adversary can count, he wins a *repique*. A repique entitles the player to add sixty to his score. Thus:—If a player has point, quint, and quatorze (all good), he repiques his adversary. He counts five for point, fifteen for sequence, making twenty, and fourteen for quatorze, making thirty-four. Instead of counting "Thirty-four," he counts "Ninety-four." In all other ways, the hand is played as already explained.

Equalities do not save a pique or a repique. In the case of an equality, the game proceeds as though no such mode of scoring existed. Thus:—A has point equal, quint and quatorze, both good, and leads a card. He wins a pique.

SCORING.

During the progress of the hand, each player continues to repeat aloud the amount of his score that hand for the time being (*see* Example, pp. 103–5). At the end of the hand, the number scored is written on a *scoring card*, each player recording both his own and his opponent's score, in separate columns.

Although the scores are, for the sake of convenience, *recorded* only at the end of the hand, they are *recordable* when they accrue, whether made by the elder or younger hand, in the order given in the following table of precedence:—

1. Carte blanche.
2. Point.
3. Sequences.
4. Quatorzes and trios.
5. Points made in play.
6. The cards.

It is important to bear in mind this order of accretion in the case of piques or repiques. Thus, a pique can only be won by the elder hand, as the card he leads counts one *in play* before the younger hand plays; hence it stops a pique. But the one reckoned by the elder hand, when he leads his first card, does not prevent his being repiqued if he has nothing good, and the younger hand can score thirty or more in hand, because scores in hand reckon before points made in play. So, also, if the elder hand scores thirty or more in hand, he does not necessarily gain a repique. Thus he may have a quint (good), a tierce, and a quatorze (good). But if his point is not good, he does not gain a repique, although he scores thirty-two in hand alone; because the younger hand's point is recordable in order before the sequences and quatorze.

To take another example: A (elder hand) has a huitième (good for twenty-six) and a tierce (good for three more). He then leads a card, and thus reaches thirty. B (younger hand) has three tens which are good. The three tens save a pique, as they reckon in order before the point made in play by A.

Carte blanche, taking precedence of all other scores, saves piques and repiques. Carte blanche counts towards piques and repiques just the same as other scores. Thus:— A player showing a carte blanche, and, after discarding, having point and quint (both good), would repique his adversary.

A capot does not count towards a pique, as the forty for the capot is added after the play of the hand is over. For instance :—A (elder hand) has ace, king, queen, knave, eight of spades; ace, king, knave, ten, eight, seven of hearts; and ace of diamonds. His point and quart are good. These, with three aces, reckon thirteen. He wins every trick, and his total score is twenty-six. He adds forty for the capot, making him sixty-six. He does not gain a pique, as he only made twenty-six in hand and play.

A player who reckons nothing that deal as a penalty (*see* Laws 25, 27, 28, 29, 31, 33, 35, 54, and 58) is not piqued or repiqued if he holds any cards which, but for the penalty, would have scored before his adversary reached thirty. His cards though not good to score, are good to bar his adversary.

A *partie* consists of six deals, each player dealing three times. The partie is won by the player who makes the higher score in six deals. If both players score the same number, each deals once more. If there is a second tie, the partie is drawn.

By agreement the partie may consist of only four deals, the scores in the first and last deals counting double. In case of a tie, each deals once more, the scores in the extra deals counting single.

The winner of a partie deducts the points scored by his opponent from his own, and adds a hundred to the difference. Thus :—A scores in the six deals 131; B scores 113. A wins 131 – 13 = 118 points. Should the loser score less than a hundred in the six deals, the winner (whether he has made a hundred or not), adds the points scored by his adversary to his own, instead of deducting them, and also adds a hundred to his score. Thus :— A scores 125; B scores 81. A wins 125 + 181 = 306. This is called winning a *rubicon*. (*See* also Laws 61–74, pp. 12–14.)

When, during the last hand of a partie, a player finds (before the play of the hand begins) that he cannot save his rubicon, he is not required to count any points in play. He throws down his hand, and tells his adversary to count every trick (thirteen), and the cards (ten). He may, if he pleases, play to divide the cards; but in that case, he has to add to his score the points he makes in play. Or, his adversary may play for a capot; but that does not affect the case, as, if capoted, the loser has no points in play to score.

Scoring cards and pencils are required. The diagram (p. 101) shows a card ruled for six parties, or for five parties if the totals are recorded on the same card.

The game is played for so much a point, or for so much a hundred, odd money not being reckoned in the final total. Thus :—A and B play five parties, at ten shillings a hundred (about equal to half-crown points at whist). A wins 75 points, as shown by the card. Fractions of fifty points are not reckoned; A wins five shillings. Some players only neglect fractions of twenty-five points; this should be agreed beforehand. Twopenny points are reckoned at a pound a hundred, fractions of

A	B	A	B	A	B	A	B	A	B	A	B
27	13	15	30	20	18	28	14	23	12	Tot	als.
15	31	75	4	4	115	11	36	9	25	150	476
44	6	45	6	10	42	22	12	40	8	416	141
18	29	32	12	33	11	8	41	15	26	126	
35	12	6	38	3	74	19	17	27	13	692	617
25	23	51	2	5	41	15	24	16	20	617	
164	114	224	92	75	301	103	144	130	104	75	
14		192			175		3	4			
150		416			476		141	126			

fifty points not counting in the final total. Threepenny points are not reckoned by the hundred, but by multiples of forty, fractions of forty points not counting; hence 75 points only score as 40. At sixpenny or shilling points, fractions of a pound are excluded in reckoning the finals; 75 points, therefore, only score as 60.

At *chouette* piquet (*see* p. 106), the points of each partie are reckoned as multiples of ten, adding one to the tens for units above five, and neglecting units from one to five. Thus, 416 counts 420; 141 counts 140. As the score must always end in a naught, the naughts are omitted when entering the figures. Taking, as an example, the parties on the scoring card, p. 101, the totals might be entered as under :—

First Partie.	Second Partie.	Third Partie.	
A + 30	A + 84	A − 96	
B − 15	B − 42	B + 48	etc.
C − 15	C − 42	C + 48	

Instead of writing each score at length, as above, and taking out the results at the end, it is found convenient in practice to add and subtract the totals after every partie, and to keep a separate scoring card for that purpose, as shown below:—

```
A + 30 + 114 + 18 + 32 + 19
B − 15 −  57 −  9 − 37 − 50
C − 15 −  57 −  9 +  5 + 31
```

A wins 190; C, 310; B loses 500. At ten shillings a hundred, when fractions of fifty points are not reckoned, A wins 150 (or fifteen shillings); C wins 300 (or thirty shillings). B, on the score, actually loses 500 (or fifty shillings); but in consequence of fractional parts of fifty points not counting in the final total of amounts receivable, B gets off with a loss of forty-five.

EXAMPLE.

The following Example will show more distinctly than mere description the mode of playing the game. The reader, if previously unacquainted with Piquet, is advised, after reading the Description of the Game (pp. 83–101), to play over the Example, and then to re-peruse the description. When playing the Example, it is advisable, in the case of learners, to place the cards face upwards on the table.

A and B are the players.

A (elder hand) has dealt him ace, king, knave of spades; ace, queen, knave, eight of hearts; knave, eight, seven of clubs; and nine, eight of diamonds.

He discards king of spades; eight, seven of clubs; and nine, eight of diamonds.

He takes in nine, eight of spades; king of hearts; nine of clubs; and king of diamonds.

B (younger hand) has ten, seven of spades; ten, nine, seven of hearts; king, queen, ten of clubs; and ace, queen, knave, ten of diamonds.

He discards seven of spades; and nine, seven of hearts.

He takes in queen of spades; ace of clubs; and seven of diamonds.

The game then proceeds thus:—
A (calls his point), "Five cards."
B (says), "What do they make?"
A (replies), "Forty-nine," or "Making nine."
B (replies), "Good"
A (says), "In hearts; and quart major."
B, "Good."
A (counting his point and sequence), "Five and four are nine." "Three knaves?"
B, "Not good."
A (leads ace of hearts, and says), "Ten."
B (says), "Four tens fourteen, and three queens seventeen." (Plays the ten of hearts.)
A (leads all the hearts, and says), "Eleven, twelve, thirteen, fourteen."
B (plays seven, ten, knave, and queen of diamonds, and, repeating his score, says), "Seventeen."
A now has five tricks, and, in order to win the cards, he should lead anything but a spade; for B, having called queens and tens, must have queen, ten of spades.
A (leads king of diamonds, and says), "Fifteen."
B (wins with ace of diamonds, and says), "Eighteen."
B (leads, ace, king, queen, and ten of clubs, and says), "Nineteen, twenty, twenty-one, twenty-two."
A (plays nine, knave of clubs, and eight, nine, of spades, and, repeating his score, says), "Fifteen."
B (leads queen of spades, and says), "Twenty-three."

A (wins with ace, and says), "Sixteen," (and then leads knave of spades, and says), " Eighteen," (and then adding the score for the cards, says), "Twenty-eight."

B (repeating his score, says), "Twenty-three."

A then writes on his scoring card, 28, 23; B writes on his card, 23, 28; the cards are gathered up by B, and the other pack is cut for A's deal.

CHOUETTE PIQUET.

Sometimes Piquet is played by three persons. The three players (A, B, C,) cut. The one who cuts the highest card (A) has choice of deal and cards, and plays one partie, *à la chouette*, against the other two in consultation. The player who cuts the lowest card (C) sits out, and advises B.

If the single player (A) wins the partie, he continues to play against the other two. C takes B's place, and B advises C; and so on.

As soon as A loses a partie, the player who advised in that partie (say C) takes A's place. B plays against the other two, and A advises C. If C loses, A takes C's place, and C advises A; if C wins, A takes B's place, and B advises A; and so on.

The single player has choice of deal and cards throughout, and plays double stakes, as at dummy.

When a *chouette* is played, the totals of each partie are recorded on a separate scoring card, as shown at p. 102.

CONDUCT OF THE GAME.

SHUFFLING.

The pack should be thoroughly shuffled after every hand. Owing to the nature of the game, cards of the same suit are often played together. Thus:—A has a sixième major in spades; B, a sixième minor in hearts. A puts down his sixième, and says, "Play six cards." B has no spade, and plays his sixième minor. A then, seeing he cannot win another trick, lays down the remainder of his sorted hand; on these cards B places the remainder of his sorted hand. Each scores seven in play. If the cards are now taken up together and are not well shuffled, the consequence will be that, when this pack is dealt again, the sixièmes will be pretty equally divided between the players, and the cards in the stock will run in suits; or if the pack is so cut that one of the sixièmes is at or near the bottom, those cards will form the major part of the stock. Even if the cards are moderately shuffled, the cards will have a tendency to keep together in suits, as any one may convince himself by giving an ordinary shuffle to a sorted pack, and then turning it face upwards.

DEALING.

The player who cuts the higher card should elect to deal. There is a slight advantage in having the first deal. The player who deals first is elder hand in the last deal of the partie, and is therefore the attacking hand when he has the best opportunity of discarding, or of playing, to the score.

MANAGEMENT OF THE STOCK.

After dealing, count the cards in the stock (and *see* Laws 10, 11, 12, 39, 40, 41, 42, and 43). Place the stock face downwards on the table, in one packet (Law 9). Some dealers separate the stock into packets of three and five. The elder hand should always object to this, as, if he takes up a card he is not entitled to see (which he might readily do if the packets happen to be separated wrongly), he can reckon nothing that deal.

TAKING UP THE HAND.

On taking up your hand, count that it contains the right number of cards; if not, announce the fact (and *see* Laws 11, 38, 39). While counting and sorting your cards, look for carte blanche.

Your next step is to decide on your discard. (*See* Discarding, pp. 116–151.)

TAKING IN.

Having discarded, you proceed to take in. When taking in, always count that you leave the full number of cards for the younger hand, the penalty for mixing one of his cards with your hand being that you can reckon nothing that deal; and this even if there is an erroneous deal, and there are not the right number of cards in the stock. The best method is to draw the stock towards you, at the same time spreading it slightly, when you can easily count the stock before taking up a card.

The younger hand, before taking in, should also count that the proper number of cards are left in the stock; if too many are left, and the younger hand mixes one of his opponent's cards with his hand, he can reckon nothing that deal.

CALLING AND SHOWING.

Before calling your hand, you should ascertain what remains good against you, or what there is equal. (*See* also p. 152.) If necessary, examine your discard for this purpose.

When a point or sequence is called, which is good or equal, it is a safe plan, especially for novices, to show it; because a player who voluntarily shows anything, which he claims to be good or equal, is liable to no penalty for miscalling (Law 55).

If you are not in the habit of showing what you call, and have put out a card of your point, which is nevertheless allowed to be good or equal, and the absent card may make a difference to your adversary in playing the cards, you should inform him of the value of the card you do not call. For example: You are younger hand, and have discarded the king of spades. You have taken in spades, and your point, which is good, is ace, knave, ten, eight of spades. When calling the point, you should say, "Thirty-nine in spades, and I do not reckon the king." Your adversary will then know, as he is entitled to know, and as he could know if he asked to see your point, that he need only keep one guard to his queen when playing the cards.

You would be equally entitled not to reckon the king, if you had it in hand, and wished to conceal your strength, in hopes of persuading your opponent to unguard his queen when playing the cards. But as calling without showing draws special attention to the absence of the king, it seems preferable always to show your point, and to say nothing about what you do not reckon. In the case supposed, put ace, knave, ten, eight of spades on the table, and say, "Good for four," and let your adversary think what he pleases about the king.

As a matter of etiquette, if, under such circumstances, you do not show your point, and do not announce that the king is out, your adversary would have just cause of complaint at not being informed. If he is misled by your ignorance of this point of etiquette, the only reparation you can make is to offer to play the cards again.

If you have, or might have, two points of the same counting value, it is also your duty to declare which of them you claim as good or equal.

Thus:—You have king, queen, ten, eight of one suit, and might have ace, queen, ten, seven of another. If thirty-eight is good or equal, you should say, "In spades," or "In hearts," or as the case may be, without waiting to be asked in which suit your point is. If younger hand, you need not announce the suit until the elder has led a card.

Similar observations apply to sequences and trios (*see* Case XII., pp. 27, 28).

If you call a trio, allowed to be good, when you might hold a quatorze of the same rank, as three kings when you might hold four, you should state which king you do not reckon, *e.g.*, "Three kings, not reckoning the king of diamonds." Many players omit to say which card of a quatorze they do not reckon, and wait to be asked. In that case, you should enquire which card of the quatorze your adversary does not reckon; but you should not put the question until he has played a card (*see*, also, Case IV., p. 22).

The question should be in this form, "Which ——— do you not reckon?" You must not assume that a card is out merely because it is not called; and your adversary is not bound to admit that he has not called a card (whether by inadvertence or design) which he holds in his hand.

If the question is put in another form, *e.g.*, "Which king have you put out?" and the adversary has not put out a king, but holds four, having called three, he is entitled to reply, "I do not reckon the king of spades," or of the suit in which he deems it best to conceal the king from you. Or, he may simply answer, "King of spades." In giving this answer, he assumes, as he is entitled to do, that you have asked him the regular question. He leaves it doubtful whether he has a king out or not; and all Piquet players understand his reply in that sense (*see* Case XVI., p. 30).

Many players have a habit of referring to the discard while the hand is being called. It is better to avoid this, as, by your consulting the discard, a shrewd adversary may gain a clue to a card you have rejected, or may be reminded of a miscall. Thus, he calls three queens, and you, having no queen in hand, immediately look at your discard. If you find a queen there, your opponent will probably conclude that you were looking for the fourth queen; if you do not find a queen there, and there has been a miscall, your adversary is reminded that he might have four queens, while he is in time to rectify his error.

PLAYING THE CARDS.

During the play of the cards, the opponent is entitled to be informed as to all the cards you have in hand, which have been reckoned as good or called as equal.

The question is usually put in this way, "How many of your point?" or, "How many of your quint?" or as the case may be. Sometimes, however, it takes this form, "How many clubs?" or as the case may be.

Suppose you hold three clubs, and have only called two of them. You are entitled to reply, "Two that I have called," or, "Two of my quint," or simply, "Two." This is understood by all Piquet players as leaving it doubtful whether you have a third club, and not necessarily that you have discarded one. The information should be only as to cards called for the purpose of scoring, or of preventing an adverse score. The enquirer is bound in effect to say, "How many of so and so have you that you have called?" (*See* Cases XV., XVI., pp. 29, 30.)

It is disputed whether a player, who has the wrong number of cards in hand, may cover his mistake by intentionally playing too many or too few to his adversary's lead. In strictness, the cards should be played one by one; but, for the sake of convenience the leader frequently puts down a number of winning cards together. If, on doing this, he says, "Keep three (or four) cards," or as the case may be, it seems only reasonable that the second to play should be at liberty to do as he is bid, and to keep the number specified. He is not bound to count the cards led by his adversary, with whom the initial irregularity rests. But, if the second to play is told to play so many cards, the case is different, and he ought not knowingly to play any other number. He must then submit to the consequences of his blunder. Some players think that even in the first instance, the wrong number of cards should not be played with intention. This is a question of ethics, which can only be decided by the custom of the card-table. No rule has ever been laid down. It is believed, after consultation with several players of repute, that the general custom is as here stated. The leader can always protect himself by counting the cards played.

Another undecided point in playing the cards, which often occurs, is this:—At the end of a hand the leader says, "All the others are yours." As a matter of fact, they are not yours, you having discarded a winning card. What is your proper course?

In the opinion of players well qualified to judge, you should make no reply to such an observation. If your adversary then proceeds to play his cards, you must play to them in the usual way, and let him win such tricks as he can. If he throws down his hand, and you have discarded a winning card, and therefore cannot win the remaining tricks, you should request him to play the cards one by one. Such a request is, no doubt, equivalent to informing your adversary that you have a winning card out, and the consequence may be somewhat disastrous to you. This is a misfortune which cannot be helped.

SCORING.

During the calling and the play of the hand, always keep in mind your adversary's score as well as your own, as, even among the most honourable players, mistakes sometimes occur. If you observe that your adversary is reckoning too much, correct him at once.

After the play of the cards, call· both your own and your adversary's scores aloud as you record them; your adversary should do the same, or should admit your call to be correct.

At the end of the partie, similarly compare the total before entering it on your scoring card (and *see* Law 74, p. 14).

DISCARDING.

INTRODUCTORY.

On account of the variety and complexity of the considerations involved in discarding at Piquet, the few general rules that can be laid down are liable to frequent modification. Subject to this condition, a statement follows of the more important points to be borne in mind when discarding.

This statement is supplemented by the application of the Doctrine of Probabilities to various cases, and by a series of illustrative Examples.

GENERAL RULES.

Before deciding on your discard, you should ascertain whether you hold anything which is good against the cards, or is equal, and what there is against you that may be reckoned as good, or called as equal.

For example:—You take up A's hand, p. 103 (*q.v.*). There are against you, a six-card point, a quint major, and four tens. You have nothing good, and may be repiqued. In addition, there are two five-card points against you, a quart minor, a tierce major, three kings and three queens. You should make yourself aware of all this before throwing out a card; and so on for other hands. At first, this will be slow work; but, with practice, you will be able to perform the mental operation of finding what there is against you, with but slight effort.

When discarding, elder hand, your main object, with moderately good cards, should be to plan an attack. You should freely unguard kings and queens, and should throw out whole suits, with a view to making a large score if you take in to the suits you keep.

On the contrary, your first care, younger hand, should be to protect your weak places. You should keep guards to kings and queens; and you should seldom denude yourself entirely of a suit of which you hold one or two small cards only, as these may guard high cards taken in. The elder hand will probably lead his best suit; and that is not unlikely to be the one in which you were originally weak. For instance:—Suppose you, being younger hand, take up the cards already referred to (A's hand, p. 103), including nine, eight of diamonds. You should not part with both the diamonds, but should discard two small clubs and one diamond.

Keeping the best suit for point is essential in most cases, and especially younger hand. The point is of much greater consequence than beginners suppose. Gaining the point makes an average difference of more than ten to the score, and, what is more important, it saves piques and repiques. It is, therefore, seldom the game for either player to discard from the suit which he selects for point.

Next in importance to the point are the cards. You should discard in such a way as to give the best chance of dividing or winning the cards Winning the cards, instead of losing them, makes a difference of about twenty-three or twenty-four points.

In consequence of the previous consideration, it not unfrequently happens, more especially elder hand, that you should not keep the longest suit for point, when that suit is composed of low cards, and keeping them necessitates the discard of high cards from other suits.

Do not break into several suits in discarding if it can be avoided. For if cards are taken in to a broken suit, it remains ragged. When you have made up your mind to discard from a given suit, it is often right to throw the whole of it. If any card of that suit is kept, it would be (*a*) because it is a winning card; or, (*b*) because it is a guarding card, more especially younger hand; or, (*c*) because it makes up a quatorze or trio.

Referring to the hand already given (A's hand, p. 103), you may discard from three suits, for the last of the above reasons, throwing out two small clubs, two diamonds, and king of spades, in order to keep the three knaves. There are four tens against you; and you have a poor chance of the point or of the cards, even if you keep the king of spades. But suppose you had the nine of hearts instead of the knave. You should then throw the clubs and diamonds, and keep two unbroken suits. Going for two suits is often the resource of a player in difficulties.

It is sometimes advisable to throw a whole suit, younger hand, either because it consists of three useless cards, or because keeping it may injure your hand in other respects. In the second case, the rejected suit should be one in which you are not likely to be attacked. Thus:—If the suit discarded consists of king, knave, and a small one, the elder hand will probably avoid leading that suit should he happen to hold ace, queen of it. King, queen, and a small card is a suit which may be discarded without much probability of being attacked in it.

It is a common error with beginners at Piquet not to take all their cards, especially if taking the full number involves parting with high cards. The hands where all the cards should not be taken are few. There is not so great an objection, however, to the younger hand's leaving a card as to the elder hand's doing so; for, in the latter case, the card left may be taken by the adversary, but, in the former case, it is merely excluded from the player's hand. The principal situation for leaving a card, elder hand, is where there is a chance of a great score, and no repique against you.

Cards in sequence, or that may form a sequence with those taken in, should be kept in preference to others of equal value. Thus:—If you are obliged to discard an ace or a king from an ace, king suit, discard the ace, as you may take in so as to hold a sequence to a king; if you discard the king you cannot hold a major sequence in that suit. But other considerations may cause you to select the king. Looking again at A's hand, p. 103, it will be seen that A throws the king in preference to the ace. His reason is that he has two aces and only one king; he may take in aces to form a trio or quatorze.

Again :—Queen, knave, ten is a better suit to keep than king, knave, ten, unless it is deemed advisable to hold a king rather than a queen. It is generally right to retain a virgin tierce to a queen, especially younger hand, unless you see a chance of a great score in other suits.

Trios should be kept if they can be retained without injuring the hand in other respects. Thus :—If about to discard a king or a queen of a suit, and you have two other kings, discard the queen; but if you have two other queens, discard the king.

It is seldom advisable to put out a high card for the sake of keeping a low trio, especially when there is a higher one or a quatorze against you. Many a hand is ruined by going for quatorzes of knaves or tens.

The discard is further affected by the state of the score, especially in the last two hands of the partie. If you are a good way ahead, and particularly in the last hand but one, if you have a chance of winning a rubicon, you should make a safe discard, with the view of dividing or winning the cards, in order to keep your adversary back. On the other hand, if the score is much against you, and you are under a rubicon, you are justified in making a bold discard. In the last hand, the discard must frequently be regulated by the state of the score.

CALCULATIONS.

The Piquet student should be acquainted with the following odds.

The odds that the elder hand (if he takes all his cards) will take in—

One named card are	. . .	3 to 1	against him
Two ,, cards are	. . .	18 to 1	,,
Three ,, ,,	. . .	113 to 1	,,
Four ,, ,,	. .	968 to 1	,,
Five ,, ,,	. . .	15503 to 1	,,
One card (at least) of two named cards are 5 to 4			,,
One ,, ,, ,, three ,,		3 to 2	on him
Two cards ,, ,, ,, ,,		6 to 1	against him
One card ,, ,, four ,,		5 to 2	on him
Two cards ,, ,, ,, ,,		3 to 1	against him
Three cards ,, ,, ,, ,,		33 to 1	,,

The odds that the younger hand (if he takes all his cards) will take in—

One named card are . . .	17 to 3	against him
Two ,, cards are . . .	62 to 1	,,
Three ,, ,, . . .	1139 to 1	,,
One card (at least) of two named cards are	5 to 2	,,
One ,, ,, ,, three ,,	3 to 2	,,
Two cards ,, ,, ,, ,,	21 to 1	,,
One card ,, ,, four ,,	29 to 28	on him

These calculations properly applied will direct the player in discarding.

Thus:—It is 3 to 1 that the elder hand does not take in a named card. It is, therefore, more advantageous to carry the best suit for point, and high cards for the chance of the cards, than to throw out any of these in hopes of taking in a card to complete a quatorze of queens, knaves, or tens (*see* Examples III., IV., and V., pp. 127–130).

The odds against taking in two or more named cards, or two of three named cards, elder hand, are so considerable, that, except in desperate cases, good cards should not be discarded on such a speculation. But the odds are very slight against taking one at least of two named cards, or two at least of four named cards; and they are in favour of taking one at least of three or four named cards.

To apply these:—If the elder hand has a quart major and two other aces dealt him, the odds that he will take in either the ten to his quart, or the other ace, are only 5 to 4 against him.

Again:—If the elder hand carries three aces and three kings, the odds against his taking either the other ace or the other king are only 5 to 4 against him.

If the elder hand has a quatorze dealt him, and there is only one superior quatorze against him, he should, as a rule, keep the quatorze, as the odds that he will take in one card at least of four named cards are 5 to 2 in his favour. But this rule may require reconsideration, with a low quatorze, if, to keep it, cards must be put out that in other ways spoil the hand, as, by compelling the player to discard from point or sequence, or to put out high cards that risk the loss of the cards, or of a capot.

With a quart to a king and two other kings, it is 3 to 2 in favour of the elder hand taking in the ace or nine to the quart, or the fourth king, and, therefore, it is very advantageous to keep the quart and the three kings.

If the elder hand has a quart to a king, and a quart major dealt him, and he is considerably behind in the score, and he must discard from one of the quarts, he should keep the quart to the king; for it is 3 to 1 against his taking in the ten to the quart major, but only 5 to 4 against his taking in either the ace or nine to the quart to the king. (For a further illustration of this calculation, *see* Example XXV., p. 144.)

The chance of taking a certain number of cards included in a larger number of named cards, must not be confused with the chance of taking a certain number of named cards. For instance, if the elder hand has two kings and two queens dealt him, the odds are 3 to 1 against his taking in two of the other kings and queens. But the odds against his taking two kings or two queens under these circumstances (*i.e.*, two named cards) are 17 to 2 against him.

The odds against the younger hand's taking in even one named card are so considerable (17 to 3 against him) that he ought not to discard on such a chance except in desperate cases (*see* Example XXX., p. 149), especially if by so doing he risks the winning or saving of the cards (*see* Example XIII., p. 135). The same rule applies *a fortiori* to more than one card.

It is only 5 to 2 against the younger hand's taking in one, at least, of two named cards. Hence, in some cases, he would discard on this chance (*see* Example XVIII., p. 139; and Example XXXII., p. 150).

Again:—It is only 3 to 2 against the younger hand's taking in one, at least, of three named cards. Therefore, if he must take in one of three cards to save a pique or a repique, it would be right for him to discard for this chance, even if, in order to do so, he must put out a valuable card, as a king, or one of his point. (For a further illustration of this calculation, *see* Example XXXI., p. 149.)

It is 29 to 28 in favour of the younger hand's taking in one of four named cards. So, having no ace dealt him, he may calculate on taking in at least one; or, with two quarts (except major or minor quarts), he may expect to take a card to make a quint; or, with a quart major against him, he may calculate on drawing, at least, one of the quart major.

If the elder hand has two quatorzes against him (say of aces and kings), it is only 33 to 31 against his drawing both an ace and a king (*i.e.*, of drawing at least one of four aces, and at least one of four kings). Younger hand, it is 4 to 1 against taking in one of each quatorze.

The younger hand has two trios, say three knaves and three tens. Either of these, if improved into a quatorze, will save the rubicon.

To keep both the trios, in good play, he must leave a card. Ought he to keep the two trios, and leave a card, or to take three cards and discard from one of the trios?

If he takes all three cards, the probability that he draws the one card to complete the quatorze is $\frac{3}{20} = \frac{57}{380}$.

If he only takes two cards, the probability that he draws one at least of the two cards to complete a quatorze is $\frac{74}{380}$.

The odds are therefore 74 to 57, or about 4 to 3, in favour of leaving a card.

EXAMPLES.

Owing to the impossibility of calculating all the chances in many cases that present themselves in actual play, differences of opinion often arise as to the proper discard. Such differences of opinion may be expressed in respect of some of the following hands. The Author will be content if he has succeeded in avoiding glaring errors, and in exhibiting a series of Examples that serve to guide those who desire to learn the game of Piquet.

The score is assumed to be love-all, unless otherwise stated.

Example I.

Unguarding a king, elder hand, to keep the point. Guarding kings, and protecting a weak suit, younger hand.

With these cards the elder hand should throw out knave, eight, seven of spades, seven of hearts, and eight of diamonds, keeping the clubs for point, and the three kings. In order to keep the point he must unguard a king; and this, being elder hand, he does not hesitate to do.

The younger hand with these cards should throw eight, seven of spades, and eight of diamonds. He should keep both his kings guarded, and should on no account part with the seven of hearts, which would be of great service should he take in king of hearts, or queen and another.

Example II.

Keeping the point. Unguarding suits elder hand, and keeping guards younger hand.

The elder hand having these cards dealt him, should keep the quart to a king for point, and the four kings, discarding queen, knave of hearts, ace, knave of clubs, and ten of diamonds.

The younger hand should also keep the point and the four kings. In addition to this he should keep all his suits guarded, and should discard knave of hearts, and ace, knave of clubs. He should not part with the ten of diamonds.

Example III.

Discarding from low trios, to keep the point.

Trios of queens, knaves, or tens, may be freely

discarded from, if, in order to keep them, a card of the point has to be put out.

With these cards the elder hand should not keep his three queens, but should throw the clubs and the diamond, and retain the other two suits unbroken.

Example IV.

Discarding from a trio, in preference to throwing from the point, or to leaving a card.

If the elder hand keeps his knaves he must either throw a card from his point or leave a card. Neither course is advisable. The general rule is not to break into the point; and it would be dangerous for the elder hand to leave a card with two seven-card points, a quint, three aces, three kings, and three queens against him. He must sacrifice the knaves to keep his point, by which means he will, at all events, divide the cards. His proper discard is the heart and the four diamonds.

EXAMPLE V.

Discarding from a trio, in order to keep the point. Going for two suits, with a better chance of the cards.

The elder hand has three queens, and there is no great score against him. Notwithstanding this, he should not part with the eight of his point (diamonds) to keep the queens, but should discard the spades and hearts. By sacrificing the queens he gives up a chance of fourteen; but by keeping the eight of diamonds he increases his chance of scoring the point, and he improves his chance of winning tricks in play.

It may be stated generally, that with ace, king, queen, and a small card of a suit, and three queens, or three knaves, or three tens not good against the cards, and such other cards that the player must either discard one of these or the small card of the point, the game is to keep the point.

Example VI.

Discarding from a point which remains good against the cards.

It is hardly necessary to state that the objection to throwing a card from the point does not apply if, after the discard, the point still remains good against the cards.

The discard, elder hand, is seven of spades, the two hearts, the club, and the diamond, for the reasons already given.

If the club or the diamond were the seven, the discard is less easy; most players would leave a card instead of throwing one of the point.

Example VII.

Discarding from low trios, to divide or win the cards. Giving up the point, younger hand, in order to keep suits guarded.

It is seldom right to throw out an ace, or a

king, in order to carry three queens, knaves, or tens, if by so doing the loss of the cards is risked.

The principal exception is when one named card taken in gives a good chance of a pique or a repique; the cards ought then generally to be risked, subject however to the state of the score, a safe discard being preferable as a rule when ahead.

The elder hand should discard the clubs and diamonds for the reasons already given.

The younger hand's discard is doubtful: on the whole, it seems safest for him to give up the point, and to discard three spades, keeping all his suits guarded, and going for the chance of queens and of dividing the cards.

In the above hand, substitute the ten of spades for the seven. The elder hand should then keep the spades and the queens. The younger hand should throw out the three clubs, unless very backward in the score.

Example VIII.

Discarding from low quatorzes, to divide or win the cards.

If the loss of the cards is risked by keeping quatorzes of knaves or tens, it is generally the game to sacrifice the quatorze. Younger hand, especially, should not put out a high card, to keep a low quatorze, when there is a superior quatorze against him.

The younger hand should discard knave of hearts, and knave, nine of diamonds. He sacrifices the knaves to keep his point, and a card of entry in every suit. By discarding thus, he must at least divide the cards; the great probability is that he will win them.

Example IX.

Discarding a quint minor, elder hand, for the chance of the cards. Keeping the quint, younger hand, as a protection against a pique.

With a quart major in one suit, a quint minor in another, and small cards in the third and fourth suits, it would generally be right, elder hand, to put out the quint minor in preference to breaking up the quart major. Keeping the quint minor will probably result in loss of the cards, *i.e.*, in a loss of over twenty points for a gain of fifteen.

But if one of the three outside cards is a knave, and the cards of the fourth suit are such that the quint minor is good against the cards, it would, in most cases, be right to keep the quint and the knaves, as the fourth knave gives a good chance of a repique.

The younger hand, in the case first stated, should not part with any of his quint. He has but little chance of saving the cards, and should throw out his three ragged cards, keeping the quart and the quint in hopes of saving a pique by his point or sequence.

EXAMPLE X.

A similar case (see EXAMPLE IX.*)*

The elder hand here should throw out the five

small diamonds, as, by keeping them, and throwing the high cards from the other suits, he would probably lose the cards, and a number of points in play. He would also give up a chance of a quatorze of queens.

It may be objected that, by discarding in the way proposed, the elder hand runs the risk of being repiqued, there being two minor quints against him. It is, however, very improbable that the younger hand can (or will), carry two minor quints.

The younger hand discard must be conceived on different principles. He must play on the defensive, and give up what small chance he has of the cards in order to make sure of saving a repique. His discard will, therefore, be ace, king of hearts, and knave of clubs.

EXAMPLE XI.

Discarding for the cards.

In this hand, the cards are of more importance than the point; the elder hand discard should, therefore, be queen and four small spades, carrying three kings and three unbroken suits. By discarding thus, if he fails to take in the fourth king, he still has a good chance of winning the cards; but if he keeps the six-card suit, and fails to take in the ace of spades, he will have a very poor chance of the cards, after having thrown out king, queen of hearts, knave of clubs, and king, nine of diamonds.

EXAMPLE XII.

Discarding for the cards.

This is a similar case to the last, but not so pronounced. Most players would discard nine of spades and king, nine, eight, seven of clubs. If the elder hand retains the point in clubs, and throws out four high cards in other suits, his chance of winning the cards is diminished. Some players prefer to discard the hearts and diamonds.

EXAMPLE XIII.

Discarding for the cards.

If the younger hand has three of each suit dealt him, and is guarded in each suit, and can calculate on dividing the cards, he should not discard more than one card, when, by so doing, he runs the risk of losing the cards. This rule applies especially when the score renders it advisable to keep the adversary back. It does not apply to cases where the younger hand, being very backward in the score, must go for a great game.

The younger hand should only take one card, discarding the seven of spades, for the reason already given.

Example XIV.

Discarding for a capot.

If the elder hand has such cards that he can win eleven tricks certain, it is often right for him to discard only one card, the losing card. Then, if he takes in to one of his guarded suits, he has a lay down capot; if not, he will very likely put his adversary to a card. No example of such a combination is necessary, as, once pointed out, the discard is obvious.

The following case applies to the younger hand :—

The younger hand should discard queen, ten, eight of diamonds, for the chance of a capot. He is not unlikely to succeed if he happens to strengthen the spade or heart suit when he takes in.

EXAMPLE XV.

Keeping unbroken suits.

Here the elder hand should throw out the five clubs, and keep three unbroken suits. He has a better chance of scoring points in play than by discarding from the other three suits.

Example XVI.

Keeping unbroken suits.

The elder hand discard is tierce minor in clubs, and queen, ten of diamonds, leaving the spades intact. It would be less advantageous to discard one diamond and one spade, as thus three suits are broken into.

Example XVII.

Throwing a whole suit, younger hand, to keep three unbroken suits.

In this case, the younger hand should throw the spades, keeping three unbroken suits, with three aces and three queens.

Example XVIII.

Keeping unbroken suits. Discarding on the chance of saving a pique.

The younger hand should discard the three small clubs, keeping three unbroken suits. He might also keep three suits by discarding the hearts; but there is a pique against him, and he ought not to part with the hearts, as they give him a chance of a quart, which saves the pique.

Example XIX.

Leaving a card.

Here the elder hand should keep his point and kings, and leave a card.

Similarly, with ace, king, and four small cards of a suit, and two other kings, the game would be to leave a card, if there is no repique against the elder hand.

Example XX.

Leaving a card.

Here the elder hand should discard nine of spades, nine of clubs, and king, queen of diamonds, leaving a card. His point, sequence, and aces are good against the cards, and he has a certain pique; but if he discards one of his hearts, he may not get the point, as there are three six-card suits against him.

The younger hand should also leave a card, throwing the two nines, and keeping his point, three aces, and the guard in diamonds.

Example XXI.

Leaving cards, younger hand.

The main consideration for the younger hand, when in doubt as to taking all his cards, is whether the card or cards taken will probably be more valuable than those thrown.

The younger hand discard is nine, eight of spades, leaving a card. If one of the guards to hearts or diamonds is thrown, a risk is run of taking in a less valuable card. By discarding only two cards and retaining the guards, the younger hand has a moral certainty of dividing the cards.

EXAMPLE XXII.

Leaving a card, younger hand.

The younger hand should throw out ten of spades, and ten of clubs, and leave a card, keeping himself guarded everywhere, and going for two unbroken suits of sequence cards.

Example XXIII.

Leaving a card with a repique against.

This, as a rule, can only be justified by the state of the score.

It is the last hand of the partie. Score: A (elder hand), 68; B (younger hand), 155.

There is a repique against B.

B discards knave, eight of clubs, and is doubtful about leaving a card. If he can make certain of not losing the partie, he should only discard two cards.

A's highest score if he carries all he possibly can, and B takes in very badly, will be 105, viz., six diamonds (good for twenty-one), a quart in hearts, and four tens (good for fourteen), which, together with sixty for the repique, score 99. He may also make six in play.

In this case B makes nine in play, and the cards, nineteen.

The scores will therefore be, A, 173; B, 174; under the most unfavourable circumstances.

B, having a certainty in hand, should not risk the partie.

EXAMPLE XXIV.

Discarding for sequence.

With two suits of nearly equal value, the one should be selected for point which gives the best chance of a sequence.

The elder hand should throw out eight of spades, ten, nine of clubs, and knave, nine of diamonds, and keep thirty-nine in hearts for point, rather than forty in clubs. The reason is, that one card, viz., the knave of hearts, if taken in, gives a quint, whereas a quint cannot be held in clubs without drawing two cards; also, by keeping the hearts, there is a better chance of winning the cards.

Similarly, a player holding ace, queen, nine, eight, seven, in one suit, and ace, knave, nine, eight, seven, in another, should keep the latter. The chance of taking king of one or the other suit is equal, and, consequently, the chance of the cards is equal; but in one case a ten taken in gives a quint, in the other it does not.

If the ten is substituted for the nine in both suits, the discard is determined on the same principle.

Example XXV.
Discarding for sequence.

The elder hand should discard nine of spades, king, queen, knave of hearts, and nine of clubs. The diamonds are kept for point in preference to the hearts, because, in the diamond suit, one of two named cards taken in gives a quint, whereas, in the heart suit, the quint can only be completed by one named card; and, whichever suit is kept, the chance of making the cards is not affected.

Example XXVI.
Discarding for sequence.

The younger hand must take in a club or a king to save a repique. He should discard queen, ten of spades, and eight of clubs, keeping two unbroken suits, both guarded, and both giving him a chance of a good sequence if he takes in a club. He should on no account discard a heart in order to keep his three tens.

EXAMPLE XXVII.

Discarding for a quatorze.

The proper discard, elder hand, seems to be quart minor in spades and ace of clubs, for the following reasons:—It is only 5 to 4 against taking queen or knave of spades. There are also two combinations in diamonds (viz., ace, ten; or ten, nine), either of which gives the elder hand a quint; and, all these circumstances being considered, there is a probability of a good score by discarding as proposed. On the other hand, if the elder hand discards the four spades only, he may leave one of the following cards: king of clubs, ace of diamonds, or, ace, queen, or knave of spades; and in any of these cases he would, probably, lose more points than by parting with the ace of clubs.

There is another way of discarding the hand, viz., by putting out the spades and one heart. By so doing, the elder hand runs the risk of putting out fourteen points on a chance which is but 5 to 4 against him, viz., of taking queen or knave of spades.

Example XXVIII.

Discarding to the score.

The discard here, elder hand, depends greatly on the state of the score.

At the commencement of a partie the discard is seven of spades, nine of hearts, and nine of diamonds, leaving two cards. Although the point as dealt is good against the cards, and is not necessarily good after the discard of the seven of spades, it is better to throw that card than to leave a third card, as, in order to repique the adversary, it is necessary to break up his septième in clubs. If the elder hand succeeds in this, his point and sequence will be good, notwithstanding the discard of the spade.

If, in the last hand of a partie, the elder hand is only playing for a pique and the cards, he should discard one of his aces (not the ace of spades), in addition to the three cards previously directed to be thrown. He thus leaves only one card, and increases his chance of breaking the septième. The fourth ace is useless at this score, as the elder hand wins the partie without it, if he takes a club.

If the elder hand only wants forty-two to make sure of the partie, his discard should be the two nines, as he can then score forty-two out of his own hand for certain. This, of course, means that forty-two wins the partie, notwithstanding the younger has a septième and makes three points in play.

If the elder hand's score is such that he must win the partie unless there is a septième against him, he should keep the spade suit and throw out the other cards.

Example XXIX.

Discarding to the score.

Before discarding, especially in the fifth and sixth hands, add up the score, and ascertain how many points each player requires.

The show of the elder hand is twenty-eight points (*i.e.*, it is about an even chance that the elder scores twenty-eight, or more); the show of the younger hand is fourteen points (*see* p. 199). By bearing this in mind, a player can easily tell whether he has the best of the partie or not. If he has, he should discard for a safe and moderate game; but, if far behind, he should make a bold discard for a pique or a repique, and should give up all consideration of winning the cards.

The elder hand, at the beginning of a partie, should discard ten, nine, eight, seven of hearts, and nine of diamonds. But if it is the last hand of the partie, and a repique is necessary to win, the discard is king of spades, tierce major in clubs, and nine of diamonds, keeping the quint and the three knaves.

Similarly, if the adversary is well ahead, in the last hand or last hand but one, a player with a quart to a queen or knave, and three queens, knaves, or tens, should make a push for the partie, by keeping the quart and the trio.

Example XXX.
Discarding to the score.

The discard of the younger hand, at the commencement of a partie, would be the three diamonds. But if, in the last hand, he were far behind in the score, he should put out king of hearts, and queen, nine of diamonds, on the chance of drawing the fourth ten, which would give him a repique. Some players would go for the repique at the beginning of a partie; but the expediency of playing so forward a game is doubtful.

Example XXXI.
Discarding to the score.

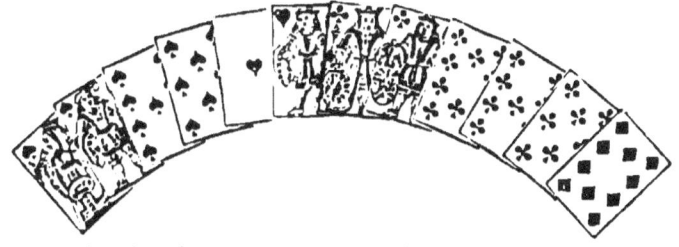

At the beginning of a partie, the younger hand should discard queen, nine, eight of spades; but

The show of the elder hand is twenty-eight points (*i.e.*, it is about an even chance that the elder scores twenty-eight, or more); the show of the younger hand is fourteen points (*see* p. 199).

ERRATUM.

Page 148, line 4; and page 173, line 7 : *for* "199" *read* "203."

and should give up all consideration of winning the cards.

The elder hand, at the beginning of a partie, should discard ten, nine, eight, seven of hearts, and nine of diamonds. But if it is the last hand of the partie, and a repique is necessary to win, the discard is king of spades, tierce major in clubs, and nine of diamonds, keeping the quint and the three knaves.

Similarly, if the adversary is well ahead, in the last hand or last hand but one, a player with a quart to a queen or knave, and three queens, knaves, or tens, should make a push for the partie, by keeping the quart and the trio.

Example XXX.

Discarding to the score.

The discard of the younger hand, at the commencement of a partie, would be the three diamonds. But if, in the last hand, he were far behind in the score, he should put out king of hearts, and queen, nine of diamonds, on the chance of drawing the fourth ten, which would give him a repique. Some players would go for the repique at the beginning of a partie; but the expediency of playing so forward a game is doubtful.

Example XXXI.

Discarding to the score.

At the beginning of a partie, the younger hand should discard queen, nine, eight of spades; but if, in the last hand of the partie, his score were eighty-three, he should go for two chances of a quint to save the rubicon, and discard knave of hearts, king of clubs, and ten of diamonds.

Example XXXII.

Discarding to the score.

At love-all, the younger hand would discard ace, nine, eight of clubs. In this hand it is more important to keep the spades guarded and the knaves than to preserve the four-card point in clubs.

Most players would make the same discard at all scores, it being very unlikely that the elder hand can carry a pique. Some, however, in the last hand, if only a pique against the hand can win the partie, would discard the spades, because then either nine of diamonds or ten of clubs taken in saves a pique. At this score the sacrifice of the knaves is of little consequence, as they are useless unless the younger hand pulls a king, in which event he is certain to win the partie.

Example XXXIII.

A doubtful discard.

This hand (elder) admits of several discards. Some players would sacrifice the knaves, and throw knave, eight, seven of clubs, and knave, seven of diamonds. Others would throw king, ten, eight of spades, seven of clubs, and seven of diamonds; or, king, ten, eight of spades, ace of hearts, and seven of diamonds; or, ace of hearts, ace, eight, seven of clubs, and seven of diamonds.

The first mode of discarding is preferred by the Author, unless the game is desperate, when the last way of discarding should be resorted to.

CALLING.

INTRODUCTORY.

Calling is not such a simple matter as at first sight appears.

Your object is to reckon all you can (except as will be pointed out), and at the same time not to expose your hand more than necessary, as by informing your adversary of the contents of your hand, you materially assist him in playing the cards.

After taking in, and before calling, look through your hand, and, if your memory is at fault, through your discard also, to ascertain what you have good, or equal, or what remains good against you.

CALLING THE POINT.

You should not thoughtlessly call your best suit for point, when you have two points. You should consider which of the two it is to your advantage to declare.

For example:—You (elder hand) have king, queen, knave, eight of hearts; and ace, queen, ten, eight of clubs. You call four cards, allowed to be good. You propose to attack in hearts; you should therefore declare that suit for point.

To carry the illustration a step further. Your other cards are ace of spades, and three diamonds.

You have put out knave, nine, eight of spades, and two diamonds.

You know, or ought to know, that thirty-eight, in hearts, is good against the cards. You call four cards, and are told that four cards are equal. Your point in clubs makes thirty-nine. But having ascertained that thirty-eight is good, you declare the point in hearts. Your adversary may then suppose that you are out in clubs, and may therefore play the cards to a disadvantage.

It may be asked, If you know your point is good, why not declare it at once?

The answer is that, when you may hold the same number of cards in more than one suit, it is generally advisable to call the number of cards of your point, even though good against the cards, in hopes of compelling your adversary to discover some portion of his hand or discard by his reply. Thus:—You have forty-seven in one suit, and might have had forty-five in another. The best point the younger hand can hold is forty-six. If to your call of "Five cards" he replies, "Equal," you know five cards in his hand; if he replies, "Good," you know he has discarded from his point.

Again:—If any four-card point which the younger hand can hold must be good, and you have a point of thirty-one, you should call three cards, though holding four. You may thus induce the younger hand to believe you have three cards in each suit, and may consequently gain several points in play. (For an example of a thoughtless call of four cards, *see* p. 175.)

REPLYING TO THE CALL OF POINT.

When you are younger hand, and the elder calls a number of cards for point, equal to yours, you should not declare the equality if his point must be good.

Thus:—The elder hand calls, "Five cards." You have already noted that the only five-card suit he can hold is ace, queen, knave, ten, eight of hearts, making forty-nine. Your five-card suit (ace, queen, knave, ten, seven) only makes forty-eight. You should not reply, "Equal" to the call of five cards, but should *at once* allow five cards to be good.

When you reply, "Not good" to a point, you should at the same time observe in which suit the call is.

For example:—Elder hand calls five cards. You have already seen that the only five-card point he can hold is in hearts. You, therefore, know five cards in his hand; this knowledge may be of great use to you in playing the cards.

Or:—Elder hand calls five cards which are equal. He may then decline to say what they make, if he knows your five cards must be better than his. Nevertheless, if he can only hold one five-card point, you know what the cards are. Or, he may declare that his cards make, say, forty-four. Forty-four is not good; all the same, you know that his point consists of five cards, without an ace, and ending in a tierce minor. You will thus probably be able to tell five cards in your opponent's hand.

The following table, if learnt by heart, will facilitate a knowledge of the cards of a point which is not good :—

A point of 34 must contain 7, 8, 9, and a tenth card.
,, 35 ,, ,, $\begin{cases} 7, 8, \text{ and two tenth cards.} \\ 7, 8, 9, \text{ and an ace.} \end{cases}$
,, 36 ,, ,, $\begin{cases} 7, 9, \text{ and two tenth cards.} \\ 7, 8, \text{ a tenth card, and an ace.} \end{cases}$
,, 37 ,, ,, $\begin{cases} 7, \text{ and three tenth cards.} \\ 8, 9, \text{ and two tenth cards.} \\ 7, 9, \text{ a tenth card, and an ace.} \end{cases}$
,, 38 ,, ,, $\begin{cases} 8, \text{ and three tenth cards.} \\ 8, 9, \text{ a tenth card, and an ace.} \\ 7, \text{ two tenth cards, and an ace.} \end{cases}$
,, 39 ,, ,, $\begin{cases} 9, \text{ and three tenth cards.} \\ 8, \text{ two tenth cards, and an ace.} \end{cases}$
,, 40 ,, ,, $\begin{cases} \text{four tenth cards.} \\ 9, \text{ two tenth cards, and an ace.} \end{cases}$
,, 41 ,, ,, three tenth cards and an ace.

For points from forty-four to fifty-one it is only necessary to add a tenth card to these. For example :—A point of forty-eight must contain eight, and four tenth cards; eight, nine, two tenth cards, and an ace; or seven, three tenth cards, and an ace. Fifty can only be made in one way, viz., with nine, three tenth cards, and an ace. Six-card points follow a similar rule; but for large points, a simpler way of finding the cards that compose them is to see whether you have in hand, or to remember whether you have in discard, the remaining cards of the suit.

CALLING SEQUENCES.

When, elder hand, you have called a point, which is equal, or not good, and you can consequently tell that your sequence in some other suit is not good, you should not call any sequence.

For instance:—Your point is forty-one, viz., ace, king, queen, ten of spades. It is not good. The only better point against you is quart major and one small diamond. Your best sequence is a quart to a queen in hearts. You should not call the quart, as it cannot be good or equal, and by calling it you only expose your hand. By not calling it, you leave it doubtful whether you have put out any hearts; and this may be of use to you in playing the cards.

SINKING.

If there is anything good against you, or equal, which is not called, you will probably be able to discover some of the cards your adversary has put out This may subsequently assist you in playing the cards.

But you must not conclude, as a matter of course, that your adversary has discarded what he does not call. Owing to the advantage in playing the cards derived from knowing the adverse hand, it not unfrequently happens that your adversary will conceal some of his cards, and not call them, although they may be good. He puts up with the loss of several points in calling his hand, on the chance of afterwards dividing or winning the cards.

You should be on your guard against this manœuvre (called *sinking*). It is especially resorted to when a player has a suit unguarded, and calling all he holds would expose the fact.

Your adversary, for instance, is a player who rarely discards from his point. He calls five cards (good against the cards), and declares five spades, when he might have six. You should immediately suspect that he may be sinking a card of his point, and should not hesitate to attack him in another suit from which he is likely to have discarded, and in which you have a tenace. The game being for him to keep his other suits unbroken, you will probably find him unguarded in the suit he has discarded.

Or:—Your adversary may hold a tierce in a suit other than his point. The tierce is good, or equal, and he does not call it. He may have put it out; or, he may be unguarded somewhere, and calling the tierce would render this evident; or, he may wish you to attack him in the suit in which he holds the tierce, and may be trying to make you think he has put out that suit.

Again:—He may have a quart to a knave, and may only call a tierce to a knave, which is good, or equal. Or, he may have a trio which he does not call; or, a quatorze, and may only call a trio.

It will be for you to judge of the probabilities in these and similar cases, and to act accordingly. You should especially suspect an experienced player of concealing cards which, if called, would reveal weakness, affecting the play of the cards, in other places.

It should be added, that it is useless to practise the stratagem of sinking cards against an indifferent player who does not count your hand.

EXAMPLES OF SINKING.

Example I.

The elder hand, having put out three small hearts and two small clubs, holds the following cards :—

His point and quart major are admitted to be good. He then proceeds to call a tierce to a king in diamonds (sinking the ten of diamonds—

this must be done without hesitation), in order to lead his opponent to imagine that the ten of diamonds has been discarded, and that the king of hearts is guarded. He then calls three kings, which are not good. He next leads the spades, and then the king of diamonds, which the adversary wins, and leads clubs. To the third club, the elder hand throws (without hesitation) the knave of diamonds, and to the fourth club, the queen of diamonds. Suppose the younger hand now remains with ace, queen of hearts, and the elder with king of hearts and ten of diamonds. If the younger hand, believing the elder to have two hearts (as would seem to him must be the case, if unacquainted with the *ruse*), leads his queen, in order to win the last trick, the elder hand makes both tricks and wins the cards.

EXAMPLE II.

The elder hand's point is equal, the younger having seven hearts. The elder also has four kings, good against the cards; but, having put out a ten, his three aces and three kings are also good against the cards.

If he calls four kings, he cannot capot his adversary. He, therefore, calls three aces and three kings, and declares that he does not reckon the king of hearts. He then leads his spades, his ace, king of clubs, and ace, king of diamonds. His adversary will have to keep one card, and, as he believes the king of hearts to be out, he will probably keep either the queen of clubs or of diamonds, and throw away the ace of hearts. If he does so, he is capoted. The elder hand gives up eleven points by sinking a king, with the moral certainty (except against a very acute or a very stupid player) of gaining thirty-two.

EXAMPLE III.

A (ELDER HAND).

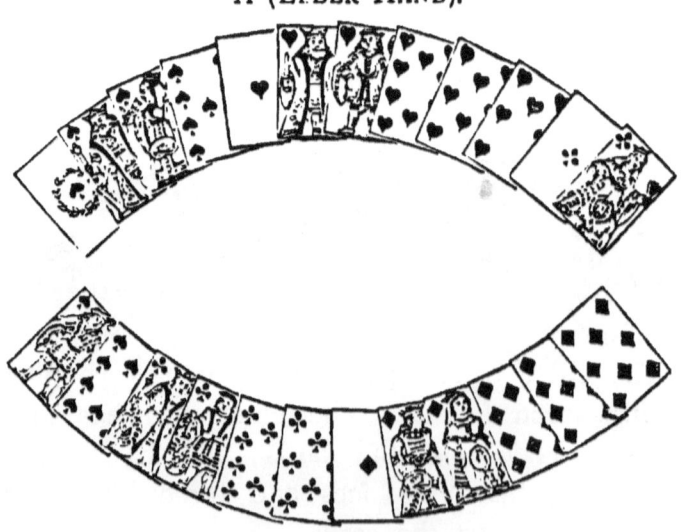

B (YOUNGER HAND).

A has discarded seven of spades; nine, seven of clubs; and knave, seven of diamonds.

A's point is not good; his tierce is equal. A does not call three aces; B reckons point, and three tens.

A leads the hearts and spades, and remains with two cards, viz., ace, queen of clubs.

B remains with king, knave of clubs, and ace of diamonds, and has yet to play one card.

If, in consequence of aces not having been called, B believes the ace of clubs to be out, he will play knave of clubs, when A will lead ace of clubs, and B will be capoted.

A *coup* such as this will generally succeed in practice; but it is difficult to see with what cards A could have gone out to justify the discard of the ace of clubs.

B is in a very awkward position. Probably his best game is to keep the clubs, as then he saves the capot, unless A has thrown four clubs and a spade, a most unlikely discard.

When put to a card, the general rule is to count the cards remaining against (*see* pp. 170, 171). There is one other consideration, viz., what cards the adversary cannot in reason have discarded. Thus:—If a player might have a quart which he does not call, and his hand is such that it would have been very bad play to discard from a quart, the presumption is he did not go out with the quart originally, and therefore that he has taken in to that suit (*compare* Example IV., pp. 162, 163).

M

Example IV.

A (Elder Hand).

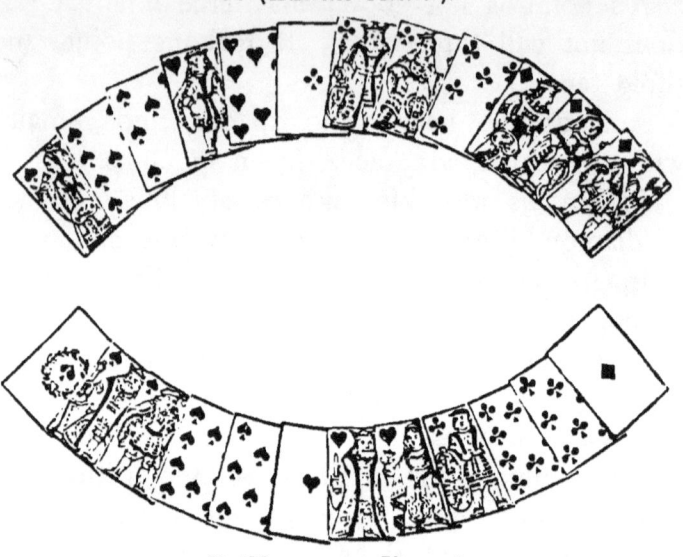

B (Younger Hand).

B has discarded nine of clubs; and ten, nine of diamonds.

A calls a point of four cards. He is therefore out in hearts and diamonds. He has probably gone for clubs and queens. The best four-card point he can hold makes thirty-eight.

B says, "Making?" A replies, "Making eight." B says, "Not good."

The tierce major is equal. B shows ace, knave, ten, eight of spades, for point, sinking the king, and reckons three aces.

A makes four tricks in clubs. To the fourth club B plays eight of spades.

A then leads king of diamonds, won by B with the ace.

B leads tierce major in hearts. To the third heart A, believing king of spades to be out, throws seven of spades. B wins all the remaining tricks.

A similar feature is to be noticed here as in the previous example. It is clear that B has a club and a diamond out. There is no conceivable combination of cards with which it would be right for B to discard a club, a diamond, and king of spades. A should see that there is something wrong; and, unless he thinks B has put out the king of spades by mistake, should keep himself doubly guarded in spades.

EXAMPLE V.

A (ELDER HAND).

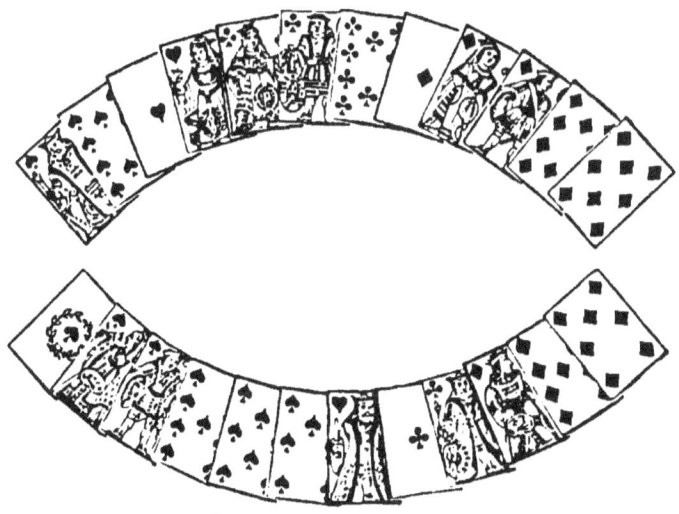

B (YOUNGER HAND).

A has discarded nine, eight, seven of hearts; and eight, seven of clubs.

He went out with the diamonds and three queens, and took in king, ten of spades; ace of hearts; and knave, ten of clubs.

B's discard was knave, ten of hearts; and nine of clubs. He kept a six-card point in spades; ace of clubs; and king, nine of diamonds. He took in king of hearts; king of clubs; and seven of diamonds.

It is the last hand of the partie. A's score is seventy-eight; B's score is a hundred and four.

It is obvious that B must win the partie, even if he does not reckon his point. All A can score, under the most favourable circumstances, is thirty-three, making him 111. B must make six in play; and this, with his three kings, good against the cards, will make him 113.

B should therefore sacrifice his score for point, as, if he can make it appear that he is guarded in hearts, and is therefore not attacked in that suit, he can divide the cards, when A will be rubiconed. A announces five cards. B might ask how many they make, and score the point, sinking one spade, if A declares hearts. B will immediately be suspected, will be attacked in hearts, and A will save the rubicon, with two tierces, nine in play, and the cards.

B should sink the whole of his point, and allow five cards to be good. He may still be attacked in diamonds or in clubs, when he at least divides the cards, and A is rubiconed.

It so happens that A's point is in diamonds. A reckons five for point, and two tierces to a queen, in all eleven.

B reckons three kings.

A leads diamonds. B wins the second trick with the king, and leads ace, queen of spades. A wins the queen, and leads the remaining diamonds, to which B throws a diamond and two spades. A, supposing B to hold king of hearts guarded, now leads queen of clubs, and B divides the cards. If B had called his six-card point, A would have led ace of hearts, instead of queen of clubs, and would have won the cards.

A scores 98, and is rubiconed.

In the worst possible case that can happen, *i.e.*, if A leads ace of hearts instead of queen of clubs, notwithstanding that B is apparently guarded in hearts, B, as already pointed out, still wins the partie.

PLAYING THE CARDS.

COUNTING THE HAND.

In playing the cards, you must be guided a good deal by what your adversary has called, and also, to some extent, by what he has not called (but *see* Sinking, pp. 156-165). You will generally know several cards in the adverse hand, or will be able to mark some that have been put out; sometimes you will know all the cards, especially after some of the tricks have been played. For instance:—If the younger hand fails to follow suit to your first lead of a suit of which you could only have five cards, it is evident he has put out three of that suit. You then know every card in his hand, and should regulate your play accordingly.

In default of actual knowledge of the contents of your opponent's hand, you should count his cards so far as he has called them, and should consider what cards he is least likely to have discarded. You then mentally assign to him the cards he has most probably kept, and so fill up his number (*see* Examples I. and II., pp. 175-177).

HABIT OF ADVERSARY.

You should also take into account the personal habit of your adversary in discarding, calling, and playing.

For instance:—Some players habitually make bold discards, and throw entire suits. These are often found unguarded. Others, on the contrary, are timid discarders. These are generally guarded, even elder hand. The timid discarder is apt to leave a card, or to put out one of his point, in order to keep himself guarded. In the latter case he may, if unguarded, have sunk a card; but timid players seldom sink anything, except in very pronounced cases.

The same division of players into bold and timid applies to their play of the cards. A timid player, for example, will never give away a chance if he can make sure of dividing the cards. Against such an adversary it would be useless to unguard a king in play (as in Examples III. and IV., pp. 178–180), because, when he finds himself with five tricks and an ace in hand, he is certain to dash out the ace.

Some, again, always throw high cards when attacked in suits in which they are guarded, in order to induce the leader to continue the suit. Thus:—With queen, nine, eight, they will throw the nine to the ace. If a player, who habitually does this, plays the eight to the ace, you may conclude he has not got the nine, and that he is unguarded.

Your safe rule as to playing small cards, is not to have any rule, and to play them sometimes in their natural order, and sometimes not.

PLAYING TO OBTAIN INFORMATION.

This presents itself in various forms. The following are two common instances.

You have ace, queen, nine, eight, seven of hearts. You decide to lead hearts, notwithstanding that your adversary has called kings, and may hold king, knave, ten of hearts.

You lead ace of hearts, to which the ten falls.

You should next lead a small heart, not the queen. You thus discover whether the knave of hearts is out.

If your adversary has not called kings, and it is possible that he has discarded a king, your second lead should be queen of hearts, as you may find the knave single against you.

Again:—Several tricks have been played, and you are in doubt what to lead. You have a suit headed by ace, king. You would generally be right to lead the ace, in order to see one more card before determining on your subsequent tactics. This point of play is of more importance than at first sight appears. It will be incidentally noticed in the Examples.

Conversely, you should play so as to avoid giving information. Thus:—When you have the choice of throwing a card you have called, or one you have not, you should prefer the former.

You have, *e.g.*, king, queen, and a small one of a suit, and have called kings, but not queens. Ace is led, to which you play the small one. The suit is continued; you should next play the king.

ESTABLISHING A SUIT.

Failing direct indications from the calling, your first lead should be from a suit you are likely to establish, such as king, queen, knave, and a small card; ace, queen, knave, and a small card, and so on. It is obvious that, when you again have the lead, you should generally pursue the suit of which you have winning cards remaining.

With two suits of equal commanding strength, you should generally begin by leading the one of which you hold the greater number. (For an exception to this rule, *see* p. 170.)

PRESERVING GUARDS AND TENACES.

When throwing to the opponent's lead, you should, of course, keep guards to kings and queens. Exceptional hands occur in which these should be unguarded, owing to the score, or to other circumstances (*see* Examples III. and IV., pp. 178–180).

When towards the close of a hand you have a tenace in one suit, and winning cards with a losing card in others, you should lead the winning cards and then the losing card, to oblige your adversary to lead up to the tenace. Of course, if you can count that your adversary is unguarded in the tenace suit, the above rule does not apply.

Also, when holding a tenace, it is often advisable to keep a losing card of another suit of which the adversary has the best, in order to give him the lead at a time when he must lead up to your tenace.

When you hold two tenace suits of equal commanding strength, and must find your adversary unguarded in one of them in order to divide the cards, you should generally first lead the less numerous suit; and, if you must play to divide the cards (owing to the score), and your adversary is equally likely to be unguarded in either suit, you should always attack first in the one of which you hold the fewer number.

The management and preservation of tenaces is a very important, and often a difficult point, in the play of the cards. (*See* Examples V. to X., pp. 181–189).

PLAYING TO SAVE A CAPOT.

When you are put to a card (*i.e.*, when your adversary has won eleven tricks and you remain with two cards, and are in doubt which of them to keep), you should keep the card of the suit of which the greater number is against you.

For example:—You remain with ace of spades and ace of hearts, and have to play one of them to a club or a diamond led. By counting all the cards played, and your discard, you find that there are three spades wanting, and two diamonds, in respect of which it is an even chance that any four may have been discarded. In that case, you should keep the ace of spades.

In making this calculation, you should include all the absent cards of each suit, without reference to the fact that one of them, which might have been reckoned in calling, has not been reckoned. For, should your adversary see he can put you to a card, he will certainly sink the combination which, if reckoned, would tell you what his twelfth card is.

An exception to this is when reckoning the score, previously assumed to be sunk, would give your adversary a pique or a repique. Then it would not be worth his while to sink a card on the chance of a capot.

PLAYING TO THE SCORE.

If you have five, or six, tricks and a winning card and the lead, play the winning card, unless *certain* that your opponent holds that suit, either from what he has called, or from the cards he has already played; for, by playing otherwise, you risk eleven points for the chance of gaining one for the last card.

If, however, one trick does not make the difference of saving, or winning, the cards, and you remain, at the end of a hand, with a winning card and a losing card, you should generally lead the losing card, in order to win the last trick, unless you can tell that the adversary has none of the suit to which your winning card belongs. For instance:—You remain with ace, queen of a suit, and the lead; and there is nothing in the previous call or play to show that your adversary does not hold the king guarded. The presumption, then, is that he has the king guarded, and you should lead the queen, in hopes of making the last trick.

These rules are liable to modification in consequence of the state of the score. For example:— Although the rule is to make sure of the cards, nevertheless, when one point saves the rubicon, or wins or saves the partie, you should risk the cards for the sake of the last trick. Again:—If you are elder hand and have the best of the partie, and can ensure dividing the cards, you should never risk the loss of them; but, if the younger hand has the best of the partie, it is often to your interest, as elder, to risk the loss of the cards, if, by so doing, you obtain a chance of winning them.

For an instance of playing to divide the cards, *see* Example XI., p. 189.

It often happens that you have the option, when playing the cards, of making a certain number of tricks off the reel, and of letting your opponent score the remainder, or of changing the lead from your hand to his, and *vice versâ*, one or more times. In either case, you win the same number of tricks; but every time you part with the lead and regain it, each player scores one point in play more than if the cards had been played without changing the lead. Whether you should make tricks straight off, or should *play in and out*, depends on the score.

If you are less than a hundred, and are not within your show (*see* p. 199), you should play in and out. If you are within your show, and your adversary is not, you should keep him back, by refraining from playing in and out.

If you and your adversary are both over a hundred, it is immaterial whether you play in and out or not. If you play in and out, for every extra point you score, your adversary does the same; so there is then no advantage to either side (*see* Examples XII. to XVI., pp. 190–196).

When you are near a pique, reckon up all the winning cards you have in hand, to ascertain whether you can make thirty before you lose the lead. If you can do so, lead your winning cards one after the other, without considering how many of the remaining tricks you will lose.

There is one exception to this rule, owing to the score. Suppose, in the sixth deal, the score is such that, if the younger hand wins the cards, he saves the rubicon. In this case, if the elder hand can win the partie without the pique, and can divide or win the cards by not leading his winning cards immediately, but would lose the cards by so doing, he should forego the pique in order to win a rubicon (*see* Example XVII., p. 197).

It may also happen, but seldom, that similar tactics should be resorted to in the fifth hand, your adversary being very backward, and you very forward, in the score.

In the last deal of a partie, if your adversary has scored less than a hundred, your object should be to prevent his reaching a hundred, and at the same time to make him score as many as possible, provided you can stop him short of a hundred. You should endeavour to prevent his declaring equalities; and if you cannot win the cards yourself, you should try to compel him to win them.

If, on the other hand, you see you cannot reach a hundred, your object should be to score as little as possible, to declare equalities, and to divide the cards. If you see you cannot divide the cards, let your adversary add thirteen (for the tricks), and ten (for the cards), to his score. You thus avoid scoring by in and out play, and score nothing, it being understood that you are not piqued or capoted in consequence (*see* p. 100 and Example XIX., p. 201).

EXAMPLES.

In the following Examples both hands are shown, for the sake of convenience. But only one hand is known, viz., the one of which the discard is stated. All that is known of the adverse hand is what is derived from calling, or from cards already played, as assumed, for instance, in Examples XII., XIII., and XIV.

The score is assumed to be love-all, unless otherwise stated.

EXAMPLE I.

Counting the hand from the call of point.

A (ELDER HAND).

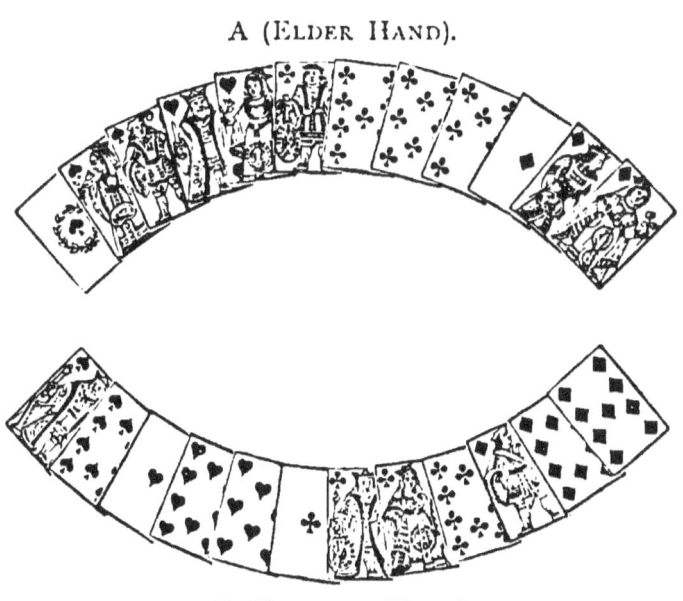

B (YOUNGER HAND).

B has discarded seven of spades; and eight, seven of diamonds.

A calls thirty-four for point, not good. The only four-card point, making four, that A can hold is in clubs (*see* Table, p. 155).

A leads the diamonds, to which B follows suit. A then leads ace, queen of spades; B plays ten, king.

B should now lead ace and another heart, when he must at least divide the cards.

If instead of leading the heart he leads the tierce major in clubs, he loses the cards.

If B could not count four clubs in A's hand, he would be right to attack in the tierce major suit. For this reason, and also because if B has a four-card point it will most probably be in clubs, A should have called thirty-one for point. In actual practice, however, a four-card point is frequently called under similar circumstances.

Example II.

Counting the hand, a trio not having been called.

A (Elder Hand).

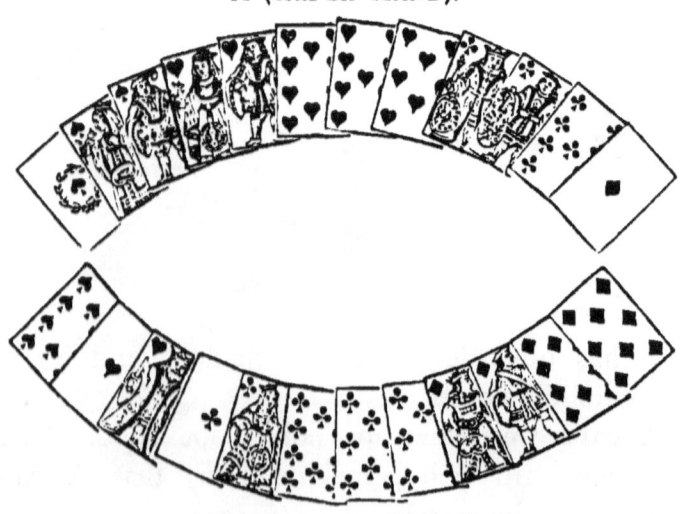

B (Younger Hand).

B has discarded eight, seven of spades; and seven of hearts.

A calls a point in hearts, a quint and three knaves, all good. He leads ace, queen, knave of spades.

A's score, in hand and play, is now twenty-six. He did not call three queens; and as these would have given him a pique, it may be assumed he has not got them.

To the spades, led by A, B therefore throws ten of spades and two clubs.

A then leads a heart. B wins it, and attacks in diamonds. However A plays, B must divide the cards.

On the other hand, if A had called three queens, B should have thrown the diamonds to the spades, and have attacked in clubs. He assigns the ace of diamonds to A as the card he is most likely to have kept, in case he went out with, say, a quart in hearts and three knaves. Under these circumstances it is more than probable that A has at least one club out, when B, by attacking in clubs, will at least divide the cards.

Experienced players may perhaps think that Examples I. and II. are too elementary to be of much use. It is, however, by considerations similar to those here given, that even the best players regulate their play in cases of greater difficulty. Beginners are recommended to observe carefully the importance of counting the hands (*see* p. 166).

Example III.

Unguarding a king during the play, in hopes of dividing the cards.

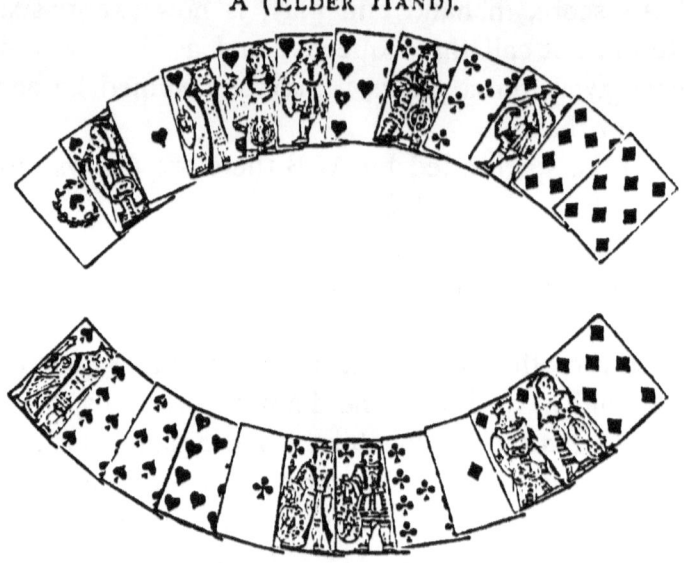

A (Elder Hand).

B (Younger Hand).

B has discarded knave of spades; and eight, seven of hearts.

A reckons five hearts for point, and a quart major. He also calls three queens, which are not good.

A leads the hearts. B plays ten of hearts, nine, eight of spades (unguarding the king), and knave, nine of clubs.

If A, now believing B to hold king, knave of spades, leads a club or a diamond, and retains his tenace in spades to be led to, he only divides the cards.

For remarks on unguarding, *see* p. 180.

EXAMPLE IV.

Unguarding a king.

A (ELDER HAND).

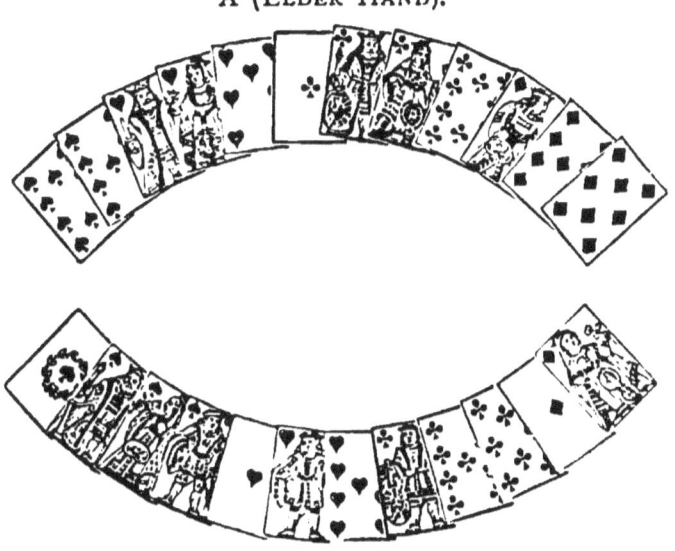

B (YOUNGER HAND).

A has discarded eight, seven of spades; ten, eight of hearts; and knave of diamonds.

A calls four cards, making forty-one. B replies, " Equal."

B reckons a quart major in spades, three aces, and three knaves.

A leads four clubs, to which B plays three clubs and a small heart.

A then leads king of hearts, won by B with the ace.

B leads four spades. A plays nine, ten of spades, and, without hesitation, eight, nine of diamonds, unguarding the king.

B then leads a heart. A makes two tricks in hearts, and divides the cards.

If it is B's habit to dash out an ace when he has five tricks, in order to make certain of dividing the cards, A's play is difficult.

A has probably asked whether three kings are good; and, if B is attentive, he will most likely count queen of hearts, and king, knave of diamonds in A's hand, and will therefore lead a heart. But if B is thoughtless, and does not take the trouble to count the hands, he may lead ace of diamonds in pursuance of his usual tactics. The worse player B is, the less likely is A's coup to succeed, and A must regulate his play accordingly.

Unguarding a king (and sometimes even a queen) during the play, if done without hesitation, will more frequently succeed against a high-class player than against an indifferent one. Of course, loss of the cards should not be risked by unguarding, unless the score renders it imperative to attempt to win them. Even then, if opposed to a player who keeps the score in view, the *coup* will hardly ever come off.

EXAMPLE V.

Lead of a winning card, to preserve the tenace in another suit.

A (ELDER HAND).

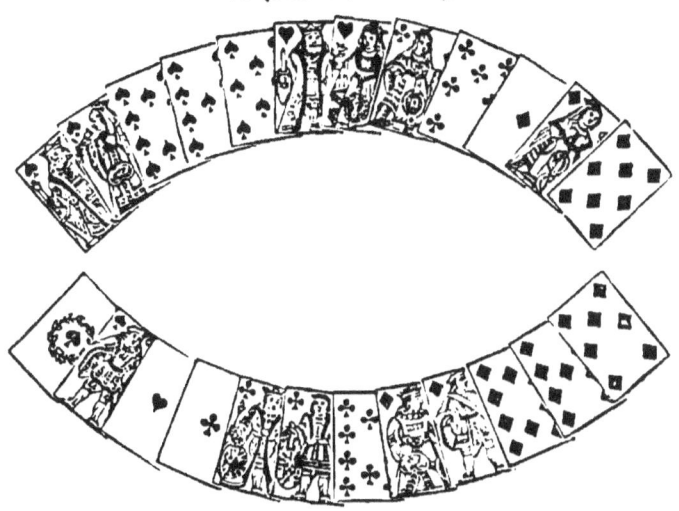

B (YOUNGER HAND).

B has discarded ten, eight of hearts; and seven of spades.

A declares a five-card point in spades, and four queens.

A leads king of spades; B wins the trick.

B leads ace, king, knave, ten of clubs; A plays seven, queen of clubs, eight of diamonds, and eight of spades.

If A plays queen of diamonds, and retains eight of spades, he is immediately attacked in diamonds, and loses the cards.

B can now read A's hand. It consists of three

spades, queen and another heart, and ace, queen of diamonds. It is possible that A has put out ace of diamonds to keep his four queens, and that he has three hearts. B need not consider this point, as then he must win the cards.

B now leads ace of hearts, that the lead may not be put into his hand again. He next leads knave of spades, when he must make a trick in diamonds, and win the cards.

If B does not get rid of the ace of hearts, A, after leading the spades, will give B the lead with a heart, and B only divides the cards.

Example VI.

Leading winning cards, to preserve the tenace in another suit.

A (Elder Hand).

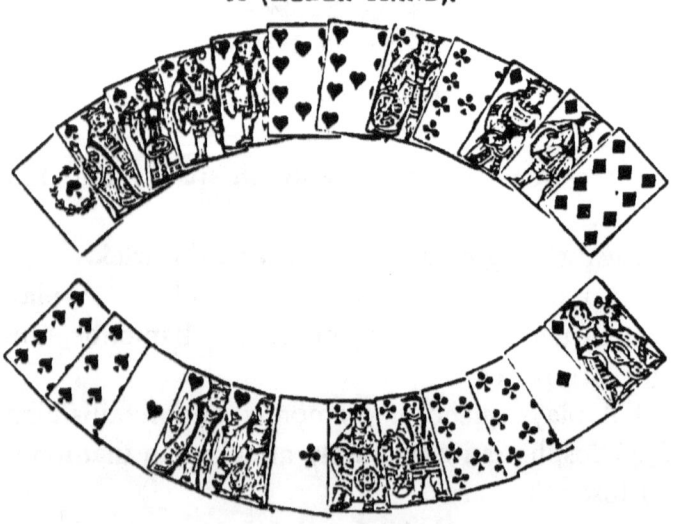

B (Younger Hand).

B has discarded nine, seven of spades; and nine of diamonds.

A calls four cards for point, not good; a quart major and a tierce to a knave, good; and three kings, not good.

B reckons five clubs for point; three aces, and three queens.

A leads a quart major in spades; B plays two spades and two clubs.

A next leads knave of hearts. B wins with queen, and leads ace, queen of clubs.

A wins the queen of clubs, and leads ten of hearts. B wins the heart, and, whatever he plays, must lose one trick in diamonds. Consequently, the cards are divided.

If B plays properly, he wins the cards. After winning with the queen of hearts, he should lead ace, king of hearts. Then, after leading ace, queen of clubs, he must be led up to in diamonds.

Of course, it is possible that A may hold a fourth heart, or a double guard to his king of clubs. In either of these cases, B can only divide the cards, however he plays.

The beginner at Piquet should keep these Examples (V. and VI.) well before him. Getting rid of winning cards in order to avoid subsequent leads is frequently overlooked by those not thoroughly versed in the game.

There is also the complementary case of reserving a losing card with which to place the lead, illustrated by Examples VII. and VIII.

EXAMPLE VII.

Keeping a losing card to throw the lead, in order to preserve a tenace.

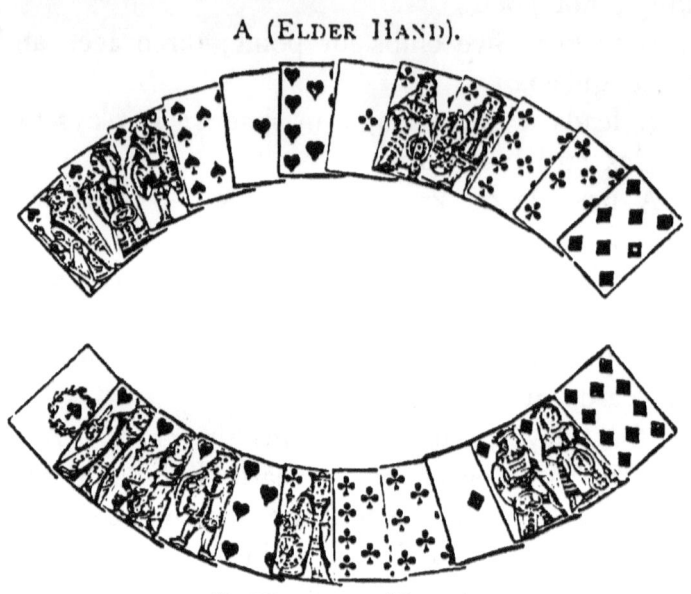

A has discarded nine, eight of hearts; and knave, nine, seven of diamonds.

A leads king of spades.

B wins it, and leads the diamonds.

To these, A should throw eight of diamonds, and three small clubs. He should on no account part with his ten of hearts.

B now leads king of hearts. A wins it, leads the spades, and then the ten of hearts, to get rid of the lead, when he divides the cards.

If A throws ten of hearts to one of the diamonds, he will remain with three clubs, one of which he must lead. He will then lose the cards.

Example VIII.

Keeping a small card to throw the lead, in order to preserve a tenace.

A (Elder Hand).

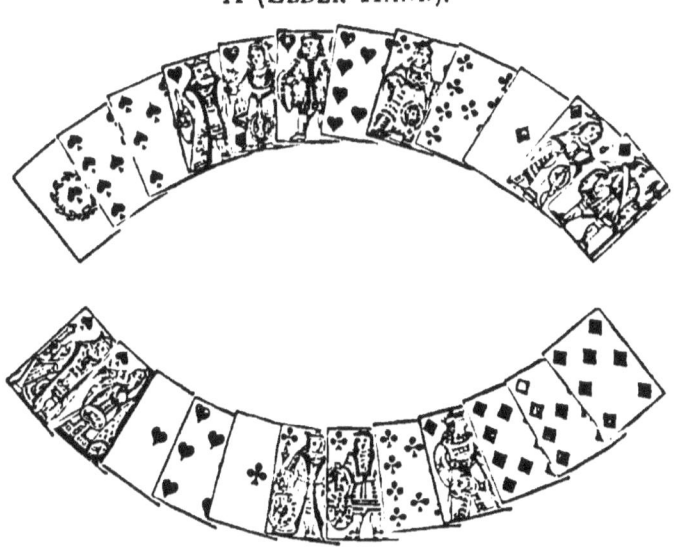

B (Younger Hand).

A has discarded knave, ten, eight of spades; and eight, seven of clubs.

A leads king of hearts.

B wins it, and leads the clubs.

To the four clubs led by B, A should play two

clubs, one spade, and knave of diamonds, keeping one small spade with which to get rid of the lead.

B next leads king of spades. A wins it, and leads the hearts, and then nine of spades. B must now lead a diamond; A makes ace, queen of diamonds, and divides the cards.

If to the fourth club, A had thrown nine of spades, he would have been obliged to continue with a diamond, and would have lost the cards.

EXAMPLE IX.

Leading the less numerous suit.

A (ELDER HAND).

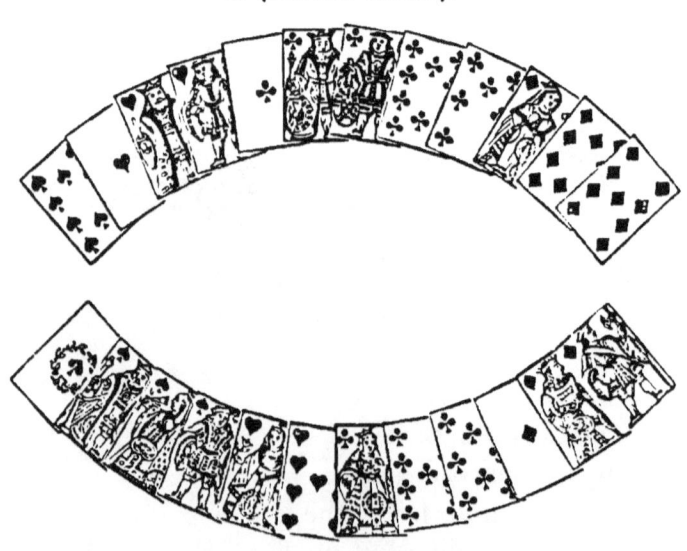

B (YOUNGER HAND).

A has discarded nine, eight, seven of spades; and eight, seven of hearts.

B has called three queens.

If B has both queen of hearts and queen of clubs guarded, he must win the cards. A should therefore play to find in which suit B is unguarded. If he begins with the club suit, of which he has five, and finds the queen guarded, he cannot save the cards. He should therefore attack in the three-card suit of hearts.

If the queen falls to the second trick, he leads the knave, and then any card except a club, and divides the cards. If the queen of hearts does not fall to the second trick, he then attacks in clubs.

Similarly, A declares a six-card point, viz., ace, queen, and four small cards. B is guarded in that suit, and holds ace, queen, ten, and two small cards of a second suit, and ace, queen, ten only of a third. As soon as B obtains the lead, he should play the ace of the suit of which he holds only three. If the adversary is guarded in that suit, he is probably unguarded in the other. If he is found guarded, B then attacks in the other in hopes of winning the cards. Should B begin with the suit of which he holds five cards, and find the adversary guarded, he has no chance of the cards, but he has a chance by playing as directed. If A is guarded in both suits B must lose the cards.

EXAMPLE X.
Leading the less numerous suit. Playing to the score.
A (ELDER HAND).

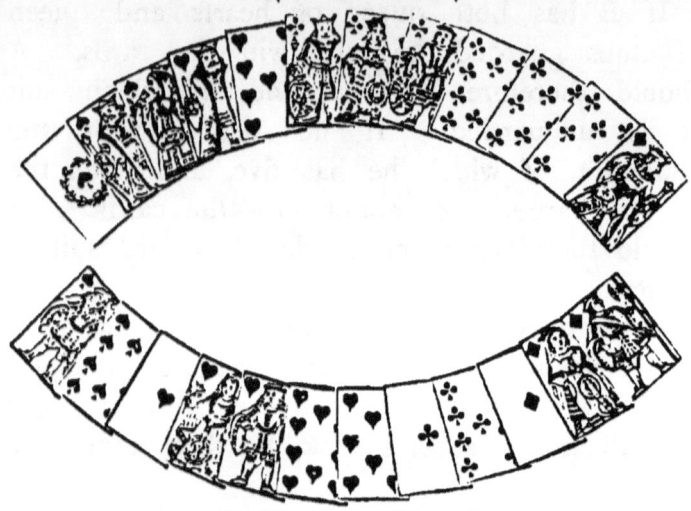

B (YOUNGER HAND).

B has discarded seven of spades; and eight, seven of diamonds.

A calls a six-card point in clubs, a tierce major in spades, and four kings. His hand is known, therefore, all but one card, and either the king of hearts or of diamonds must be unguarded.

A leads tierce major in spades. B plays two spades and eight of hearts. He must not part with his nine of clubs.

A now leads king of clubs, which B wins.

B should lead the ace of diamonds, because it is his less numerous suit. If the king falls, he continues the diamonds, and then leads nine of clubs, and divides the cards.

If the king of diamonds does not fall to the ace, B next leads hearts, and divides the cards.

If B leads ace of hearts, before the diamond, and finds the king guarded, he loses the cards; but if he finds the king of hearts unguarded, he wins the cards. B's play may therefore depend on the score. If winning the cards wins the partie, or saves the rubicon, B should risk the heart; if dividing the cards wins the partie, B should lead the diamond. Or, if B is considerably behind in the score, and winning the cards brings him within his show, he should generally lead the heart (*see* Example XI.).

EXAMPLE XI.
Making sure of dividing the cards.
A (ELDER HAND).

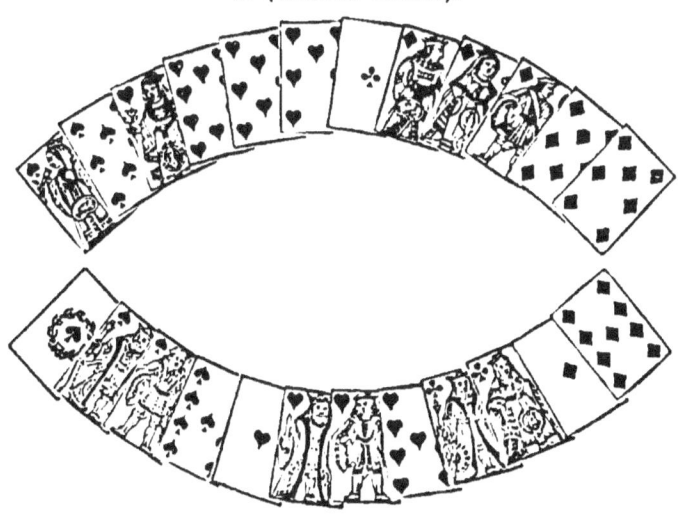

B (YOUNGER HAND).

B has discarded knave, ten of clubs; and ten of diamonds.

A declares five diamonds, and leads the king. B wins the trick.

The probability is that A has gone for diamonds and queens. It is not at all unlikely that he has queen of spades or queen of hearts single.

B therefore leads ace of spades. A plays the eight. B still makes an effort to win the cards, and leads ace of hearts, to which A plays the seven.

B is quite in the dark as to the remaining spades and hearts in A's hand. As it happens, if B pursues the attack in hearts, he loses the cards. On the other hand, if A has guards in spades instead of in hearts, and B continues to attack in spades, he also loses the cards.

Under these circumstances, B can make certain of dividing the cards by now leading king of clubs. If the score is such that he must play to win the cards, he has no alternative but to continue his attack at random in one or other of his ace, king suits.

Example XII.

In and out play.

The last three cards in the leader's hand are king, queen, ten of a suit, of which he can count the adversary with ace, knave, and a small one.

The leader makes certain of three points in play by leading the ten. If he leads king or queen, he only scores two, should his adversary refuse to win the card first led.

In one case, the score in play is A, two; B, three. In the other, it is A, three; B, four.

A's proper lead depends on the score (*see* pp. 172, 173).

Again:—A has tierce major, and two small spades; and, king, queen of diamonds.

B has called four knaves and three aces.

A leads four of his spades. If knave of diamonds remains in B's hand, A makes seven in play by next leading a diamond. But, if A leads the fifth spade, and knave of diamonds is thrown to it, he only scores six in play.

EXAMPLE XIII.

In and out play.

A has, declared in his hand, ace, queen, knave of spades; and king, ten of hearts.

B holds, ace, queen, knave of hearts; and king, ten of spades.

It is the last hand of the partie. A, who is ninety-five, leads the ace of spades, which makes his total score ninety-six. A has already won three tricks (excluding the ace of spades), and B four.

If B throws the king of spades to the ace, A can only score to ninety-nine.

If B throws the ten to the ace, each player makes one more point in play.

The card for B to play to the ace depends on the score Thus:—If B requires four points to save the rubicon, he should play the ten to the ace.

Example XIV.

In and out play.

A has, declared in his hand, ace, queen, knave of spades; ten of hearts; ace, nine of clubs.

B holds, king, ten of spades; knave, nine of hearts; king, queen of clubs.

A can count B's hand, and knows him to be singly guarded in both spades and clubs.

If A leads ace, queen of spades, he will score five in play, and B will score four.

The result will be the same if A leads ace, nine of clubs.

If A leads ten of hearts, he scores six in play, and B five. The number of tricks won by A will be the same in either case, viz., three.

After what has already been said, it will be clear that A's lead depends on the score.

Say it is the fifth hand of the partie, and that A is under a rubicon. He should lead the heart.

Or, to take an extreme case, it is the last hand, and A's score (including what he has already made in the hand) is ninety-four. If he does not lead the heart, he is rubiconed.

On the other hand, if A is well ahead, and his game is to keep B back, he should not lead the heart.

EXAMPLE XV.
In and out play.

A (ELDER HAND).

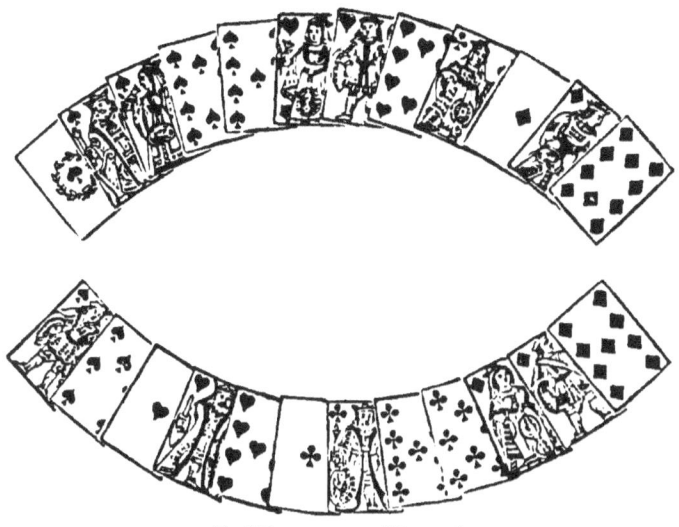

B (YOUNGER HAND).

B has discarded eight of spades; and eight, seven of diamonds.

A scores seventeen in hand (point in spades, tierces in spades and hearts, three queens, and three tens).

He must win the cards, and he requires, in addition, ten in play to get out of the rubicon.

All the cards in his hand, except two, are known from the call. It is highly improbable that he has put out both ace and king of diamonds, especially as he does not reckon the ten of clubs. Therefore, it may be assumed that he has at most two clubs. In that case, he cannot make more than nine in play, if B plays properly.

A leads the spades. To these, B plays two spades and three diamonds. A then leads three diamonds, and any other card, and only scores nine in play. B scores five in play.

On the other hand, if B requires six to save his rubicon, he should keep the diamonds guarded, and should throw to the spades, two spades, a heart, and two clubs. If then he leads a diamond when he gets in, he scores one more in play. A scores two more in play; but B has succeeded in saving the rubicon.

Example XVI.
In and out play.

A (Elder Hand).

B (Younger Hand).

A has discarded nine, eight of spades; nine, eight of clubs; and ten of diamonds.

It is the sixth hand of the partie. A has only four aces good, which bring his score to seventy-seven. He wins the cards, and has to reckon thirteen in play to save the rubicon.

B's point is in hearts. A can score thirteen by in and out play, unless B has three diamonds, and attacks in that suit. Even if B has three diamonds, it is unlikely he will lead them until obliged, as he may find A with ace, queen, ten of the suit.

A leads seven of hearts; B plays the nine. If, instead of the seven, A leads ace, king of hearts, as he probably would in an ordinary hand, he cannot reckon thirteen in play.

B leads anything—say, queen of hearts. A wins with the king, and leads ace, eight of hearts. It is compulsory on A to lead eight of hearts after the ace.

B wins the eight of hearts, and next leads a club, which A wins.

A's best lead is now seven of spades. B wins with the ten, and continues the club. A wins it, and must return the seven of clubs.

If B now leads a spade, A wins it, returns the spade, and then leads queen of diamonds. Or, if, instead of a spade, B leads a diamond, A wins it, and leads ace, queen of spades, and makes the last trick with a diamond.

The reason A leads seven of spades, at the

sixth trick, instead of going on with the club suit, is now apparent. Suppose all the hearts and clubs played, and that A remains with ace, queen, seven of spades, and ace, queen of diamonds. B has king, knave, ten of spades, and king, knave of diamonds, and it is B's lead. B leads a diamond, won by A. A leads seven of spades, won by B, who again leads a diamond, won by A.

Now A remains with ace, queen of spades, and is in a dilemma. He cannot tell whether B has two spades left, or a spade and a diamond. If then A leads ace of spades, on the speculation that B has one spade and one diamond (the probable case), he fails to score thirteen in play. By leading the seven of spades at an earlier period of the hand, as directed, A avoids being thus put to a lead.

At some scores, A's play would be very bad. As played, A reckons thirteen and B ten. By leading three aces and two kings, and any other card (keeping ace, queen of diamonds), A makes the same number of tricks, but the scores in play are, A, nine; B, six; a difference of four to each player. Suppose then B were ninety-three after counting his hand, and A any higher score, A should not play in and out.

Or, suppose it is the fifth hand of the partie, and that A can reach the score of eighty-six, by playing in and out. He should play to get within his show (*see* p. 173).

EXAMPLE XVII.

Playing to the score, and foregoing a pique.

A (ELDER HAND).

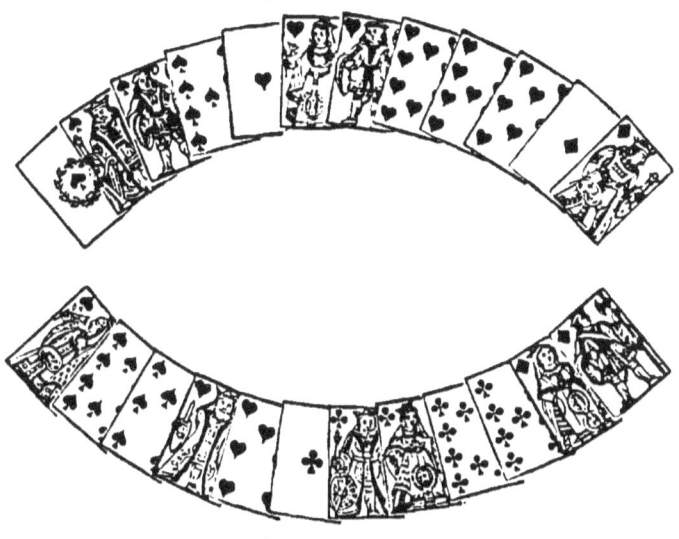

B (YOUNGER HAND).

It is the last hand of the partie. A has discarded knave, eight, seven of clubs; and ten, eight of diamonds.

A's score is seventy; B's score is eighty-two.

A has a pique, good against the cards, if, after reckoning his point, quint, and three aces, he leads his aces and kings, and then any other card.

If A plays in this way, he scores sixty, and his total score is a hundred and thirty. B scores eight in play, and ten for the cards, and his total score is a hundred. B saves the rubicon, and A wins a partie of a hundred and thirty.

But, if A foregoes the pique, and leads ace and another heart, he must divide the cards, whatever B has discarded. A then wins a rubicon.

Played in this way, with the hands given above, A scores twenty-four in hand, two in play (for ace, queen of hearts), and six for the last five tricks (in all thirty-two), and the cards are divided.

B scores seven in play (this he must reckon in order to divide the cards).

The scores will then be, A, a hundred and two; B, eighty-nine. A wins a rubicon of two hundred and ninety-one.

By foregoing the pique, A gains a hundred and sixty-one points.

In order to avoid complicating the case with other considerations, the question of A's best play has hitherto been neglected. It will be seen that A can still make sure of dividing the cards if he leads the ace of spades before attacking in hearts. And, he may find B unguarded in spades. In that event, he wins a pique and the cards. If the queen of spades does not fall to the ace, A should then change to the heart suit, leading ace and queen as above advised. In other words, A should not thoughtlessly throw away a chance of a pique, because he sees he can certainly win a rubicon by foregoing it.

EXAMPLE XVIII.

Playing to the score, and sinking point and quatorze to win a capot.

A (ELDER HAND).

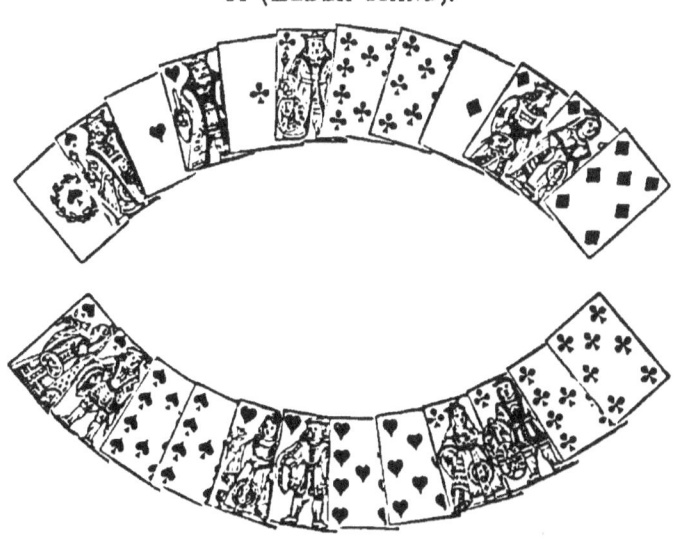

B (YOUNGER HAND).

It is the sixth hand of the partie. The scores are, A, forty-three; B, ninety.

A has discarded eight, seven of spades; ten, seven of hearts; and nine of diamonds.

If A's point of thirty-nine in clubs is good, B must be out in spades, and A scores a repique.

If B is out in spades, A can equally win a repique by calling a point of thirty-eight in diamonds. In either case B is rubiconed.

On the other hand, if B has his quart in spades, there is no repique. A's resource, then, is a capot, and this he can win if B is unguarded in clubs.

But A may possibly capot his adversary, even if guarded in clubs, by inducing him to believe that clubs are out, elder hand. If A calls thirty-nine for point, it is evident that the point is in clubs, and B will keep himself guarded in that suit. A's object, therefore, should be to conceal the fact that he holds four clubs, and A should call thirty-eight in diamonds. It has already been shown that, if B has four spades, this call can only injure A to the extent of four points, a matter not worth considering as against the chance of a capot.

B replies, "Not good." He therefore has a quart in spades.

A, in pursuance of his tactics, calls four kings and three aces (not reckoning the ace of clubs).

A leads his four diamonds. To three of the diamonds B plays nine of spades, eight of hearts, and seven of clubs. B has now to play one other card. If he believes the ace of clubs to be out, he will naturally throw the nine of clubs. If he does so, he is capoted.

The scores will then be:—A, seventeen in hand, thirteen in play, and forty for the cards and capot; total, seventy. This, added to his former score of forty-three, makes him a hundred and thirteen. B scores eight, making him ninety-eight. A wins a rubicon of three hundred and eleven.

EXAMPLE XIX.

Playing to score as little as possible, and to divide the cards.

A (ELDER HAND).

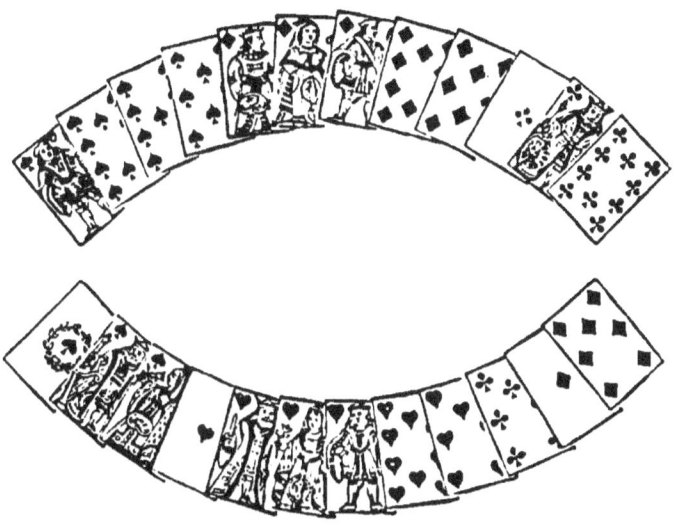

B (YOUNGER HAND).

It is the sixth hand of the partie. A has discarded nine, eight of hearts; and queen, nine, eight of clubs.

B's score is fifty.

A's first care should be to see whether B can possibly make fifty, which saves the rubicon. Whatever he has discarded, he cannot score more than forty-seven.

If A calls, "Forty-eight" in diamonds, B will reply, "Equal," and will declare forty-eight in hearts, his object being to declare equalities. A should call twenty-nine for point, which compels a score. B should allow this to be good.

A should then call a quart to a knave. B should say, "Not good," as, if he admits it, A also reckons a tierce in diamonds.

A then calls three tens, which B, in order to conceal his hand, allows to be good.

A leads ace of clubs, that he may not risk being put to a card; and, as he cannot win the cards, should try to lose them. A next leads king of diamonds.

It is now B's turn. He has discarded seven of spades; knave of clubs; and nine of diamonds. In order to reckon as little as possible, he only calls a quart in hearts.

B wins A's diamond; and, if he plays properly, can divide the cards.

B leads tierce major in spades, four tricks; ace, king of hearts, six tricks. To the hearts A plays king of clubs and ten of diamonds, endeavouring to lose the cards if B holds knave of clubs or nine of diamonds.

B now leads seven of diamonds. A wins it with the knave; and, as he has only winning cards in his hand, the cards are divided.

If A had continued with a second club after the ace, B should have thrown the ten of hearts, as seven of hearts and seven of diamonds, if kept in hand, may enable B, after winning six tricks, to get rid of the lead when A remains with only winning cards.

ODDS AT PIQUET.

THE SHOW.

The *Show*, elder hand (when small cards are counted in play), is twenty-eight; younger hand is fourteen. That is, it is about an even chance the elder hand will score twenty-eight or more, and that the younger hand will score fourteen or more.

The above results have been obtained empirically thus:—

In 10,000 hands—

	The Elder Hand scored	
	28 or more	27 or less
Times	5129	4871

It is therefore slightly in favour of a score of at least twenty-eight, elder hand.

In 10,000 hands—

	The Younger Hand scored	
	14 or more	13 or less
Times	4997	5003

This gives fourteen as the show, younger hand.

The show, when small cards are not counted in play (as was formerly the case), is twenty-seven elder hand and thirteen younger hand. It is not known how this result was arrived at. It is believed that it can only be obtained by the laborious method of keeping statistics of a large number of hands, as has now been done for the rubicon game, in which small cards are counted in play.

ODDS AT VARIOUS SCORES.

The odds at various scores may be deduced approximately from the following tables:—

In 10,000 Hands, the Elder Hand scored	
Under 10	977 times
Between 10 and 20	1743 ,,
,, 20 ,, 30	2867 ,,
,, 30 ,, 40	2105 ,,
,, 40 ,, 50	902 ,,
,, 50 ,, 60	76 ,,
,, 60 ,, 70	166 ,,
,, 70 ,, 80	664 ,,
,, 80 ,, 90	106 ,,
,, 90 ,, 100	20 ,,
,, 100 ,, 110	88 ,,
,, 110 ,, 120	210 ,,
,, 120 ,, 130	40 ,,
,, 130 ,, 140	2 ,,
,, 140 ,, 150	18 ,,
150 or more	16 ,,

In 10,000 Hands, the Younger Hand scored	
Under 10	3556 times*
Between 10 and 20	2560 ,,
,, 20 ,, 30	2317 ,,
,, 30 ,, 40	944 ,,
,, 40 ,, 50	423 ,,
,, 50 ,, 60	35 ,,
,, 60 ,, 70	13 ,,
,, 70 ,, 80	21 ,,
,, 80 ,, 90	5 ,,
,, 90 ,, 100	28 ,,
,, 100 ,, 110	52 ,,
,, 110 ,, 120	38 ,,
,, 120 ,, 130	7 ,,
,, 130 ,, 140	0 ,,
,, 140 ,, 150	0 ,,
150 or more	1 time

To Work the Tables.—Add together all the hands which score less than the amount required; and separately add together all the hands which score the number required or more. The sum of the one, as against that of the other, will give the required odds approximately.

Examples.—(1). It is the last hand of a partie. The elder hand is 90. Required the odds in favour of his saving the rubicon.

The odds are 9023 to 977, or nearly $9\frac{1}{4}$ to 1 that he will score 10 or more.

* Of these, 102 times he scored 0.

(2). Required the odds that the elder hand will score at least 20.

The odds are 7280 to 2720, or about 8 to 3 in his favour.

(3). It is known to be an even chance that the elder hand will score 28 or more. It is therefore slightly against his scoring at least 30. The tables give 5587 to 4413, or about 5 to 4 against.

(4). The odds against the elder hand scoring 40 or more are, according to the tables, 7692 to 2308, or about 10 to 3.

(5). It is the last hand of the partie. The elder hand is 140 points behind. Required the odds against the elder hand's winning the partie.

The odds given by the table are 9966 to 34, or 293 to 1. The elder hand must get a repique and capot to win. In a few cases, the younger hand may score a quatorze, when he may win, notwithstanding the elder hand's repique and capot. Making a full allowance for this contingency, the odds are about 290 to 1.

(6). In less desperate cases, the calculation of the odds becomes rather more complicated, as the consideration of the score made by the younger hand has to be taken into account. Thus:—It is required to find the odds that the elder hand will score 90 more than the younger.

This cannot be discovered from the tables; but it may be approximated to as follows:—

Including the cases in which the elder scores between 90 and 100, the odds against him are about 24½ to 1. Excluding these cases, the odds are about 25 to 1. It may be concluded that the odds against the elder hand are nearer to 25 to 1 than 24 to 1.

As the odds against a repique are 27½ to 1, and as an elder hand repique does not necessarily score 90 more than the younger, it might be argued that the odds should be more than 25 to 1. But more than 90 may be scored without a repique, as by pique and capot. And, on looking at the table, it will be seen that the elder hand scores over 100 more than eighteen times as often as he scores between 90 and 100. Hence it would seem that the odds of 25 to 1 are not far from the mark.

(7). Required the odds that the younger hand will save the rubicon, he being 90, last hand of a partie.

The odds are 6444 to 3556, or 9 to 5 in his favour.

(8). The younger hand wanting 20 to save the rubicon, the odds against him are 6116 to 3884, or about 13 to 8.

NEGLECTED VARIATIONS.

The tables necessarily neglect variations which may arise in consequence of discarding and playing to the score, the great majority of the recorded hands having been played without reference to these considerations, and all hands having been omitted in which a player, finding his game hopeless, has played to divide the cards, or to score as little as possible.

The odds found by the tables can only be regarded as *approximate* odds, and as less than the true odds against a player who has to gain a point for which he especially strives. For instance:—The elder hand wanting 29 to get out, and seeing it on the cards to make that number, might discard, or play the cards, accordingly. On the other hand, the odds may be more than the true odds against a player who has the partie well in hand, and who is only scheming to keep his adversary back, as, *e.g.*, when the elder hand sacrifices a pique in order to win or to divide the cards.

ODDS IRRESPECTIVE OF THE TABLES.

It is about 5 to 3 on the elder hand for the cards; nearly 3 to 1 against the younger hand's winning the cards; and a trifle over 7 to 1 against the cards being divided.

The odds against a rubicon are about 7 to 2. The odds against a named player being rubiconed are, therefore, 8 to 1.

A partie averages two hundred points.

The odds against a repique elder hand are nearly 27½ to 1; against a younger hand repique, about 75 to 1.

The odds against a pique (which of course includes a repique) are rather more than 7 to 1 (about 36 to 5).

The odds against a carte blanche in a named player's hand are 1791 to 1.

THOS. DE LA RUE & CO'S LIST.

PUBLISHED BY THOS. DE LA RUE & CO. LONDON,
AND SOLD BY ALL BOOKSELLERS.

WORKS BY "CAVENDISH."

THE STANDARD WORK ON PATIENCE.
Demy Oblong 4to. Cloth, Gilt. Price 16s.

PATIENCE GAMES.
WITH EXAMPLES PLAYED THROUGH.
Illustrated with numerous Diagrams, printed in Colours.

THE STANDARD WORK ON WHIST.
22nd Edition (80th Thousand). *8vo. Cloth, Gilt Extra. Price 5s.* Greatly enlarged and revised throughout. Handsomely printed in Red and Black.

THE LAWS & PRINCIPLES OF WHIST.
4th Edition. *8vo. Cloth, Gilt Extra. Price 5s.* Handsomely printed in Red and Black.

WHIST DEVELOPMENTS:
AMERICAN LEADS & THE UNBLOCKING GAME.

4th Edition. 8vo. Paper Covers. Price 6d.

AMERICAN LEADS SIMPLIFIED.

8vo. Cloth, Gilt Extra. Price 1s. 6d.

WHIST PERCEPTION.
ILLUSTRATED BY END-HANDS FROM ACTUAL PLAY.
BY "B. W. D." AND "CAVENDISH."

THE STANDARD WORK ON PIQUET.
9th Edition. 8vo. Cloth, Gilt Extra. Price 5s. Greatly enlarged and revised throughout. Handsomely printed in Red and Black.

THE LAWS OF PIQUET,
Adopted by the PORTLAND and TURF CLUBS. With a TREATISE ON THE GAME, by "CAVENDISH."

4th Edition. 8vo. Cloth, Gilt Extra. Revised throughout. Price 2s. 6d.

THE LAWS OF ÉCARTÉ,
Adopted by the TURF and PORTLAND CLUBS. With a TREATISE ON THE GAME, by "CAVENDISH."

2nd Edition. 8vo. Cloth, Gilt Extra. Price 1s. 6d.

ROUND GAMES AT CARDS.
BY "CAVENDISH"

PUBLISHED BY THOS. DE LA RUE & CO. LONDON,
AND SOLD BY ALL BOOKSELLERS.

3rd Edition. 8vo. Cloth, Gilt Extra. Price 1s. 6d.

THE LAWS OF RUBICON BÉZIQUE.

Adopted by the PORTLAND and TURF CLUBS. Edited by "CAVENDISH."
WITH A GUIDE TO THE GAME, BY "CAVENDISH."

9th Edition. 8vo. Cloth, Gilt Extra. Price 1s. 6d. Greatly enlarged and revised throughout.

THE GAME OF LAWN-TENNIS
(WITH THE AUTHORIZED LAWS). BY "CAVENDISH."

THE POCKET SERIES.
By "CAVENDISH." Price 6d. each.

WHIST (5)—Guide; Laws; Leads; Rules for Play of Second Hand
Rules for Play of Third Hand.
PIQUET. BÉZIQUE (with New Laws). RUBICON BÉZIQUE.
POLISH BÉZIQUE. ÉCARTÉ. CRIBBAGE. EUCHRE. IMPERIAL.
SPOIL-FIVE. CALABRASELLA. DAAMA, or Turkish Draughts.
SIXTY-SIX. DOMINOES. CHESS. DRAUGHTS. BACKGAMMON.

THE STANDARD WORK ON BILLIARDS.
6th Edition. Carefully revised. Crown 8vo. Cloth. Price 10s. 6d.

BILLIARDS.
By J. BENNETT, RETIRED CHAMPION. EDITED BY "CAVENDISH."
With upwards of 200 Illustrations.

CLAY ON WHIST.
Improved Edition. Cap. 8vo. Cloth, Gilt Extra. Price 3s. 6d.

LAWS OF SHORT WHIST,
By J. L. BALDWIN;

AND A TREATISE ON THE GAME,
By JAMES CLAY.

5th Edition. Revised and Augmented. Cap. 8vo. Cloth, Gilt Extra. Price 3s. 6d.

THE PHILOSOPHY OF WHIST.
By DR. POLE, F.R.S.
An Essay on the Scientific and Intellectual Aspects of the Modern Game.

By the same Author. Handsomely printed on a Card. Price 3d.

PHILOSOPHICAL WHIST RHYMES.

May be had of all Booksellers and Stationers.

RUBICON BÉZIQUE

(With the AUTHORIZED LAWS) as played at the
PORTLAND and TURF CLUBS,

WITH A GUIDE TO THE GAME.

BY "CAVENDISH."

Four Packs of Bézique Playing Cards and Bézique Markers
(with Table of Scores), etc., etc.

In a great variety of neat and ornamental Cases.

Prices from 5/- to 60/-

PIQUET.

WITH A GUIDE TO THE GAME.

BY "CAVENDISH."

Two Packs of Playing Cards and Two Scoring Blocks, etc.

In a variety of Leather Cases.

Prices from 8/- to 25/-

RUBICON BÉZIQUE AND PIQUET.

In handsome Leather Cases, containing

THE TWO GAMES COMBINED.

Prices from 42/- to 70/-

WHOLESALE ONLY OF

THOS. DE LA RUE & CO.

BUNHILL ROW, LONDON.

MANUFACTURED BY THOS. DE LA RUE & CO.
AND SOLD BY ALL BOOKSELLERS AND STATIONERS.

PATENT "PNEUMATIC" PLAYING CARDS.
EASY SHUFFLING.   PERFECT DEALING.

The Fronts of the "Pneumatic" Playing Cards are highly finished, whilst the Backs are minutely grooved or indented all over the surface, so as to provide an air-space between the cards, and a roughened surface which acts as a resistance for the thumb in dealing. This PREVENTS MISDEALS, as the cards slide off one by one and can be dealt with the greatest ease and rapidity.

PATENT PLAYING CARDS.
MOGULS (or BEST QUALITY), HARRYS (or SECOND QUALITY), and the cheaper kinds of HARRYS and HIGHLANDERS, with Round or Square Corners, in great variety.

The round-cornered cards are cut by improved machinery to an absolute uniformity in size and shape.

"DEXTER" PLAYING CARDS,
EXTRA THIN.

WITH PATENT INDEX-PIPS, ROUNDED CORNERS, AND ENAMELLED FACES.

"PIGMY" PLAYING CARDS.
BEST QUALITY.   HIGHLY ENAMELLED BACKS, IN ASSORTED TINTS. Adapted for the Game of "PATIENCE."   Price 1*s.* per Box of Two Packs.

"PATIENCE" PLAYING CARDS.
INDEX-PIPS, BEST QUALITY, HIGHLY ENAMELLED BACKS, IN ASSORTED TINTS.
In a variety of styles.   Prices from 2*s.* 6*d.* per Box of Two Packs.

"MIDGET" TOY PLAYING CARDS.
TINTED BACKS, ASSORTED.   IN NEAT TUCK CASES, PRICE 2*d.* PER PACK.

BÉZIQUE PLAYING CARDS,
IN BOXES, FOR TWO, THREE, OR FOUR PLAYERS.
With Markers, and "GUIDE" by "CAVENDISH."
In a great variety of styles.   Prices from 2*s.* 6*d.* to 63*s.*

In neat Cardboard Case, Price 6d.   In handsome Leather Case, Price 2s.

"INDEX" DOMINOES (REGISTERED).
HANDSOMELY PRINTED IN BLACK AND GOLD.

On highly-finished Cardboard, with the Indices in the left-hand corners.

A NEW AND AMUSING DIVERSION FOR YOUNG AND OLD.
Price One Shilling.   Entered at Stationers' Hall.

WORD-MAKING AND WORD-TAKING.
EACH BOX CONTAINS OVER 300 LETTERS.
Printed on highly-finished Enamelled Cardboard, with Rules of the Game.

A CHEAPER ISSUE, PRICE SIXPENCE,
CONTAINING HALF THE ABOVE QUANTITY OF LETTERS.

PUBLISHED BY THOS. DE LA RUE & CO., LONDON,
AND SOLD BY ALL BOOKSELLERS AND STATIONERS.

DE LA RUE'S
INDELIBLE DIARIES
AND RED-LETTER CALENDARS.

POCKET DIARIES.
DE LA RUE'S IMPROVED INDELIBLE DIARIES AND MEMORANDUM BOOKS, in four sizes, in a great variety of bindings.
A size, 3¼ by 1¼ in. B size, 3¾ by 2½ in. C size, 4½ by 2¼ in. D size, 5¾ by 3½ in.

CONDENSED DIARIES AND ENGAGEMENT BOOKS,
In three sizes (A, B, & C, as above), in a great variety of bindings.

PORTABLE DIARIES.
B size, 3¾ by 2½ in. D size, 5¾ by 3½ in.
Thin, light, and flexible, in a variety of leather cases. Adapted for the Pocket.

HALF-CROWN DIARY.
DE LA RUE'S IMPROVED DIARY AND MEMORANDUM BOOK; for Library or Counting-house use. E size, 7½ by 4¾ inches.

POCKET CALENDARS.
DE LA RUE'S RED-LETTER CALENDARS AND ALMANACS, in two sizes (A & B, as above), suitable for the Card Case or Purse.

"FINGER-SHAPED" DIARIES.
In elegant sliding cases, extra gilt. Adapted for the Pocket or Reticule.

"THUMB-SHAPED" DIARIES.
In elegant sliding cases, extra gilt.

"PALM-SHAPED" DIARIES.
In elegant sliding cases, extra gilt.

WALL, TABLET, OR EASEL CALENDARS.

THE "NOTA BENE" STYLOGRAPH
(PATENTED)

Is ready for Instant Use. May be carried in any position without fear of leakage. Holds a Large Supply of Ink.

5/-

In Polished Vulcanite, Handsomely Enchased. With Needle, Spring, and Nozzle, made of the Precious Metals.

5/-

MAY BE HAD OF ALL STATIONERS.

"PELICAN" SELF-FEEDING PEN
(PATENTED)

Writes Instantly and Continuously.
Has Extra Large Reservoir of Ink.
Secure against Leakage.
Flow of Ink to the Pen can be regulated with the greatest nicety.

10/6

In Polished Vulcanite,

Handsomely Enchased.

Fitted with a Barrel Pen of Special Construction, in 14-carat Gold, Iridium-Pointed.

10/6

"SWIFT" RESERVOIR PENHOLDER
(PATENTED)

3/6   **3/6**

Holds a large supply of Ink; ready for instant use.

The construction of the Holder affords absolute security against leakage, and preserves the Ink for any length of time. Cannot corrode or get out of order, being made entirely of hard vulcanite.

Fitted with Iridium-Pointed Non-Corrodible Pen	....	3s. 6d.
" Union Gold Pen, Iridium-Pointed	....	5s. 6d.
" Superior " "	....	10s. 6d.
" 14-Carat " " and Gilt Mounts	....	12s. 6d.

Refills:—Iridium-Pointed Gold Pens, 2s. 6d. each; ditto, Best Quality, 5s. and 7s. 6d. "Swift" Non-Corrodible Iridium-Pointed Pens, 6d. each.

Wholesale only of the Sole Manufacturers,

THOS. DE LA RUE & CO., Bunhill Row, LONDON, E.C.

THE "ORB"
GOLD-COATED ACID-RESISTING PENS.
FINE, MEDIUM, BROAD, AND EXTRA BROAD.

Box containing One Dozen, 1/-

Card holding ½-Dozen, Assort? Points 6d.

These Pens are made of a Non-Rusting Alloy, Plated with Real Gold, and possess excellent Writing Qualities.

THE "ORB"
CONSTANT SERVICE FOUNTAIN PENHOLDER
(PATENTED)

2/6 IN FINELY POLISHED HARD VULCANITE. **2/6**

CARRYING AN ACID-RESISTING NIB, GOLD-COATED.

SPECIAL ADVANTAGES:—

Carries an unusually large quantity of Ink.
Does not require any adjustment before use.
Pen-nibs of an inexpensive character may be used, and can be easily replaced.
When empty, may be dipped and used as an ordinary Pen.

MAY BE HAD OF ALL STATIONERS.
Wholesale only of the Sole Manufacturers,
THOS. DE LA RUE & CO., Bunhill Row, London, E.C.

MAY BE HAD OF ALL STATIONERS.

"ISOBATH" CONSTANT-LEVEL INKSTAND
(PATENTED)

AUTOMATIC IN ACTION.
SECURING UNEQUALLED ADVANTAGES.

SECTION, SHOWING CONSTRUCTION

Adapted for all Countries and all Climates.

Made in a variety of useful and ornamental forms.

The Float is so weighted and poised as always to keep the Ink on the same level, whatever quantity may be contained in the Reservoir. The Mechanism cannot get out of order, as all the materials used are entirely unaffected by Ink.

Has a large Reservoir of Ink, enclosed from dust and evaporation, and a small Dipping-Well in which the Ink is always maintained at the same level.

The INK IS ALWAYS READY; ALWAYS OF THE RIGHT DEPTH for dipping; ALWAYS FRESH and CLEAR for use.

PRICES from 2/6 to 45/-

THE PATENT "ISOBATH" CONSTANT-LEVEL MUCILAGE JAR.
Fitted with Brush and Cap, complete, Price 6/-

THE PATENT "ISOBATH" CONSTANT-LEVEL STAMP & ENVELOPE DAMPER.
PRICE 10/6

By Royal Letters Patent.

THE "CAVENDISH" WHIST MARKER.
THE "CAVENDISH" PIQUET MARKER.
THE "CAVENDISH" BÉZIQUE MARKER.

Price One Shilling and Sixpence.

THE "SIMPLEX" POCKET WHIST CASE.
This Case is constructed with Markers recessed in the back, and contains a Pack of superior Playing Cards and a Card of Whist Rules.

MAY BE HAD OF ALL STATIONERS.

PATENT REVERSIBLE PEN-CLEANER
SOLE LICENSEES: THOS. DE LA RUE & CO.

Prices from
1/- each.

Size, 4¼ × 3½ inches.

Reversible Pads
FOR REFILLS
2d. each.

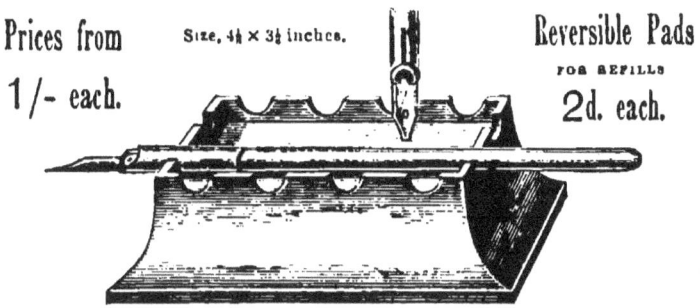

The Pen, when not in use, should be thrust into the Pad perpendicularly, as shown in the cut. The Pad may be reversed, when soiled from long use, by pushing it out from the bottom. When the base is screwed to a desk, for Public use, the Pad may be prised out readily from the top. Can also be used as a Pin-cushion.

Wholesale only of the Sole Manufacturers,
THOS. DE LA RUE & CO., Bunhill Row, LONDON.

RANSOME'S PATENT
POCKET INKSTANDS.

These compact and convenient Inkstands are sold in the four sizes given below, and will be found very suitable for the Pocket or Travelling Bag. Their construction secures them from leakage and from the liability to be upset when in use.

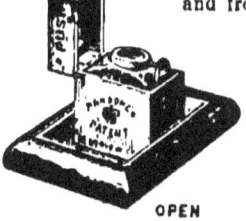
OPEN

SHUT

Metal Frame	Size, 2¼ × 1¼ in.	... ...	5s. 0d.
Polished Walnut Frame	″ 2⅜ × 1¾ ″	... ...	5s. 0d.
″ ″	″ 2⅞ × 2⅜ ″	... ...	7s. 6d.
″ ″	″ 3⅜ × 2¾ ″	... ...	10s. 6d.

Wholesale only of the Sole Agents,
THOS. DE LA RUE & CO., LONDON.

www.ingramcontent.com/pod-product-compliance
Lightning Source LLC
Chambersburg PA
CBHW021013240426
43669CB00037B/877